My Life As A Church Planter

A SPIRITUAL JOURNEY BY

Douglas Snowsell

I lift up my eyes to the mountains—
where does my help come from?
My help comes from the Lord,
the Maker of heaven and earth.

[Ps 121:1–4 NIV]

Robert
God bless the work of your hands

Doug

Produced by:

FriesenPress

Suite 300 – 852 Fort Street
Victoria, BC, Canada V8W 1H8

www.friesenpress.com

Distributed to the trade by The Ingram Book Company

Table of Contents

In his second book Doug Snowsell shares extraordinary missionary experiences that have resulted not from personal greatness but from learned obedience and submission to the greatest One of all. You will be carried from ecstasy to exasperation, from joy to tears as you vicariously come face to face with a life worth living—a life dedicated to a God worth following

Personal regards,
Preston Manning

Life is an interesting journey and when you are an International Worker it is filled with unique experiences that are both exhilarating and challenging to the core. Doug Snowsell does a masterful job in telling the story of his personal journey as an International Worker in South America. His honest reflects provide a raw look at not just the work of those who serve in other countries but the emotional challenges that accompany that work. One of the marker moments in the book was when Doug answers the question, "What do you actually do as a missionary?" He writes, "If pressed to answer what we did as missionaries I answer we were church planters, although I am not sure to this day what that means. One of my mentors used to encourage us by asking "Do you know how to plant a forest? The question demands a negative response. However when it is rephrased as a series of questions starting with, "Do you know how to dig a hole?" Can you put a tree in that hole?" You realize that you could, given enough time, plant a forest." This commitment to do the next thing that God required is echoed throughout the manuscript. I was challenged by the stories and inspired by the honest reflections of down to earth ministry. I would highly recommend this book.

Rev. David Hearn
President of the C&MA in Canada

You are about to read the REAL LIFE account of an ordinary man who has an amazing and meaningful life experience. Doug and his wife have not feared the unknown though many times tested on their next adventure in life and in travels.

Doug Snowsell and I grew up in small town Kelowna, British Columbia, Canada back in the 50's. We went to school together. But, as each of us had opposite interests in life after graduation went our separate ways following graduation. Doug became a banker and worked his way through the small, medium and large branch systems of Western Canada advancing his career quickly. Doug then had a sudden about turn, left banking having discovered a greater calling. In his first book BANKING ON BELIEVING he wrote about his earlier banking years and his first taste of a new calling as a Missionary. This change in life and purpose transformed his way of life and his belief system. Indeed, an interesting, compelling and absorbing reading experience.

Doug Snowsell's Mission 'mid life and beyond' has taken him to very interesting places and meeting very interesting people. This World Traveler, in his second literary outing MY LIFE AS A CHURCH PLANTER shares the same raw, honest portrayal of a very interesting man In fascinating places, often under unusual circumstances with interesting, often unpredictable people. Doug's word pictures of his life and experiences are so vividly scribed.

Doug's meeting with President Pinochet of Chile, Doug's discovery of the majestic Andes. Being assaulted by terrorists, Travels to the headwaters of the Amazon. And, the profound experience of establishing a world-wide Ministry to support marriages ALMA.

MY LIFE AS A CHURCH PLANTER also shares Doug's wife Ann's memoirs from their 36 years of marriage Share this easy read about the Journey of Doug and Ann in their pursuit to do good for God and Mankind. This book expresses humour, fear, joy, tears, and the extraordinary. MY LIFE AS A CHURCH PLANTER is a book hard to put down once you begin. And, that's what a good literary experience should be like. MY LIFE AS A CHURCH PLANTER does not disappoint.

Walter Gray
Mayor of Kelowna
School Chum - KSS

Preface

A letter to my children, Brandon and Colin and my grandchildren, Charlotte Ann Snowsell and Elliot Douglas Snowsell.

This family history has been in my heart for many years now. I first thought about putting it down in writing after your Grandmother Ann passed away. There was too much pain, too much change, too much everything and it overwhelmed any possibility of my writing at that time. She loved you both even before you were born.

Out of my profound respect for Ann, who was the writer in our family and whose gifts for writing the boys have received, I have left her work largely untouched. I realize there are errors as her pieces were never meant to be included in a book. Rather they are what she called *trip letters*, and I feel that her personality is best represented in the original form.

After your birth, Charlotte Ann, the urge to write returned. I remember the day of your dedication, dear one, and the words of Psalm 121. My paramount desire was, and is, that you soon know the God of your Grandmother Ann so that you also can walk in His protection, His leading, His new life.

Those new feelings soon began to materialize in my mind as a continuation of the thoughts Ann had recorded in her *Heritage of Miracles*; a legacy for her boys—all three of us. Nancy is now very much part of my history, but your mother, Brandon James and Colin David, and your grandmother, Charlotte Ann and Elliot Douglas, is your true family heritage.

Why now? Why, after all these years, bring up feelings from a past perhaps well left alone? The first answer that comes to mind arises as a result of conversations I have had over the years with Brandon regarding my recollections and times he tried to correct me, saying things like, "Dad, you exaggerate," or "Dad, it really wasn't like that." Approaching my seventieth year, I want to tell the stories my way. Cut me some slack if your memories are slightly different from mine.

There are events recorded here that you boys never knew about or, as a result of what is recorded here, you will understand better. Your mom and I made many mistakes in your upbringing. Never did we make one because we didn't love you or want the best for you. I cannot ever describe the pain we carried due to our family being separated in order to facilitate our mission in Chile—never.

Also, I want to make our story available to the many hundreds of supporters of the ABCD Snowsells, who through their giving and their prayers made themselves very much part of our story and our family. Thank you.

The final and most important response to *'why now'* is the acknowledgement of eternal gratitude and love to my God. I shudder to think what my life—and subsequently your lives—would have become without Him, had He not reached out to rescue me time and time again. To my Saviour, I owe my life—without Him this story would be of a life wasted rather than a life well lived.

Douglas Snowsell
March 2010

Introduction

I was born in 1943 to second generation fruit farmers in Kelowna, British Columbia in the lush Okanagan Valley.

When I was fourteen, my father succumbed to health complications stemming from his confinement in a German POW camp. I learned then that tragedy is often the beginning of greater things. When I grew up, I forsook the family tradition of farming and began a new life in the world of corporate banking.

I had no idea that, after sixteen years and a successful career, circumstances would again intervene and set me on a new path. I left my banking career, its corporate perks and pension, in order to follow a life of faith and new beginnings.

After four years of study at CBC/CTS in Regina (Canadian Bible College/Canadian Theological Seminary) my wife, Ann, and I plus our two children, Brandon and Colin, ventured out on an entirely new career. We moved to San José, Costa Rica, to attend language school for a year in preparation for our future work in Chile.

We finished our language training August 1982 very excited yet our family was under a pall because we'd have to part from our sons in Quito at the Alliance Academy which would be their home for the next few years.

We stayed with them in Ecuador for two weeks and helped them settle in, personalize their rooms and explore Quito. The day we left them we gathered in a football huddle in Brandon's room. My recollection is blurred by emotion and fogged with tears but I recall crying out to God and demanding that He hear my plea, "Father, we may never again be a normal family. I beg you to keep us a united family even though we are separated by hundreds of miles."

Ann and I believe that God honoured my request. In fact we share something that perhaps only missionaries share—the indescribable joy of being together again. The first time the boys came to Chile was at Christmas. We put all our mattresses on our bedroom floor and talked until the dawn light was in the sky. When we went to sleep we all snuggled on the floor.

The farewells were never easy. One time at Santiago Airport we were there with another missionary family. We all stood paralyzed on the observation deck and watched the plane disappear into the haze. We asked the other family—they had raised five children in Chile and had been in the country for 37 years—"Does it get any easier?" They replied tearfully, "No."

All of this was covered in greater detail in my first book entitled *Banking on Believing*. We pick up the action in August of 1982, as Ann and I arrive in Pinochet's Chile.

PART ONE: Chile 1982–1990

Viña del Mar 1982–1984

Early Days

We arrived in Chile in August of 1982. In the southern hemisphere, winter was just ending, and we felt the cold after living a
full year in the tropics. We were graciously housed, together with
our four large suitcases, in the guest room of our new colleagues,
Gordon and Jan.

Within days they began our orientation, which included a
two hour trip to the coastal city of Viña del Mar. We arrived to
a huge bank of fog that had rolled in, hiding the ocean view and
most of the city. We were assured by our hosts that, "The ocean is
right there and it is beautiful!" I don't know when our suspicious
natures were aroused, but it could have been at that moment.
There seemed to be an agenda of which we were not yet aware.

In the next few days, we were to learn that the Mission wanted
to assign us to an English- speaking Scottish Presbyterian Church
in Viña, knowing full well that our heart's call was to the capital
of Santiago.

Allow me to explain why we knew we were to work in Santiago:
at that time there was no work amongst the middle and upper

class in Chile; my banking experience qualified us to feel comfortable with these people; and close to eighty percent of all Chileans lived within a hundred kilometres of Santiago. I consider myself a very pragmatic thinker, and the current mission concept of going to the hinterlands made no sense to me when we could concentrate our efforts where the people already were. Nothing we said would convince the Mission leaders. At one point I believe I even appealed to our Canadian leaders, but we were wisely told to toe the line.

When talking with us didn't seem to change our minds, we were invited to a meeting of all the Mission leaders in Temuco, located in the sparsely populated south of Chile, which was the headquarters of the Mission and the National Church.

If they were trying to impress us, that was certainly not the way. Temuco is much farther south, and in the southern hemisphere that means *colder*—there was frost there! Our Costa Rican bodies shivered. In addition to that, the dear couple who had volunteered to be our hosts had run out of money that month and had no heat in their house. They did have an electric blanket, and we stayed in bed just as long as possible without appearing to be rude.

The next day we were summoned to the Mission headquarters to face the leaders. It felt like the inquisition. Ann and I were seated on two chairs facing the others. The case was presented as to why we should go to Viña del Mar. What they didn't know was that God had already helped us make our decision. He had told us, days earlier, that we were to obey our leaders and leave our future in His hands.

On and on they pontificated , like good lawyers presenting their case. At the end of what seemed to be hours, they said, "We will adjourn now and give you time to pray about it, and you can give us your decision tomorrow."

The next day, with our unreserved approval, we were immediately assigned to the Scottish Presbyterian church in Viña del Mar.

The Wedding

In November of 1982, Bruce and Joan, the missionaries we were to fill in for, left for their year at home. Soon after that we were visited by the head elder of Union church, a retired Admiral of the Chilean Navy.

Although a fourth-generation Chilean, Gerald could not have been more English. To be appreciated the following conversation it has to be heard with an upper-class English accent, which to my wife's chagrin I began to mimic.

"How are things?" Gerald asked.

"Fine," I said. "Thank you very much."

"Is the house comfortable? Do you need anything else?"

"No everything is just fine. Thank you very much."

Gerald smiled then said. "Do you like the new car?"

"Yes," I said. "Very much."

At this point I was getting tense because it was evident this was not just a social visit.

"Very good," he said. "Yes well, I have something to tell you. It seems there is going to be a wedding."

"Is that so?" I was cautiously optimistic—my mind racing and praising God for His incredible mercy. I had never conducted a wedding. *How good of God to provide me such an opportunity.*

My optimism was short-lived.

"Yes," he said. "It will be in Spanish of course . . ."

Now I am speechless. As Gerald relayed some of the details, my burgeoning terror was, I am sure, visible on my face. I am certain it affected this very proper English gentleman who couldn't have stood to see a grown man cry; the final detail was revealed only as he turned and strode out of the house.

"Oh and, by the by," said Gerald in full retreat, "the President and his *junta* [cabinet] will likely be there."

In an instant I realized why they keep missionaries very poor. President Pinochet and his top government officials would be in attendance to watch a poor tongue-tied, novice pastor perform his first wedding ever. Simply put, if I had had the resources at that time, we would have purchased tickets and fled home.

The wedding took place on a Saturday evening, January 8th, 1983. The story is best told by Ann in her letter to our boys.

Taken from *A Heritage of Miracles*

> *Many times when we were struggling to learn Spanish in Costa Rica, we wished God would give us the gift of tongues—SPANISH.*
>
> *He didn't then, but there was one day in January 1983 when He most certainly gifted Daddy!*
>
> *You remember how we got to Viña. Just after arriving, Daddy was informed that he would be performing a wedding in January, between the daughter of a retired Admiral of the Chilean Navy and the son of the Minister of Interior of the Chilean government. We were told that President Pinochet was likely to attend—but none of this was as intimidating as the fact that the wedding would be in Spanish! Here we were—first term missionaries—only six months away from bungling along in language school.*
>
> *Nevertheless, Daddy faithfully prepared a sermon, had it corrected grammatically by our language tutor, and practiced with him by the hour—reading and reading, trying to get the pronunciation correct. He did what he could.*
>
> *That Saturday in January was a beautiful summer day. I've never known horror to take place in sunshine, but that day was one of increasing horror as the hour approached.*
>
> *Finally, around six o'clock (the wedding was at 8 p.m.) we couldn't stand it anymore, so we got dressed and walked down to the church. We decided we could*

take pictures of the flowers and maybe just calm our nerves a bit. But when we got a block away from the church, we found it cordoned off by plainclothes policemen! That sure didn't help the nerves. Luckily they believed who we were and let us pass. When we got to the church we found it already 25% full—with more police! So dear Dad just went behind to the pastor's study, in a desperate attempt to calm down.

The church holds 300—there were 800 present—filling every nook and cranny and spilling outside. The President was to arrive at 8:05 and the bride 5 minutes later. The President arrived on time. After 5 minutes, Daddy stood up in front of everybody to wait for the bride. She didn't come. I can't remember how late she was, but it was long enough for stark terror to penetrate every fiber of poor Daddy's quivering being. It was a hot summer evening. There were 800 people staring at him, including the President, and he knew that soon he was going to have to speak Spanish. However, he consoled himself with the thought that the opening hymn would be in English and that would give him confidence. Well, the bride finally came and then came the hymn. But the terror only increased—because Daddy's mouth was so dry that not a single croaking sound came forth. Then the hymn was over Daddy began. And so did God! When it came time for the sermon, Daddy was speaking fluidly and flawlessly. I sat there in utter amazement—I had heard him practicing dozens of times, and he had never even come close to doing it as well as he was doing now. The people listened with great interest, and even chuckled at the appropriate places! It was awesome!

Finally it was over, and my suspicions were confirmed—it was great! One lady said, "There are missionaries who have been here for over 20 years and can't speak as well." Many congratulated him, but the highlight was when one member of the Junta asked the Minister of Interior why he had never met this Chilean before! When Daddy spoke, he didn't even have an accent!

Now you boys speak better Spanish than we do. We see you wince as we mutilate a word with our mispronunciation. But on this one occasion, your dad spoke miraculous words—every word guided, formed, breathed on by the God of miracles who wanted these 800 people to hear and hear clearly the message of Jesus. It was truly a gift from God!

Back in Viña, the Mission must have been aware of how much free time we had. Our assignment had arisen out of the need to fill in for Bruce and Joan, the missionary couple who were presently pastoring the church. They left for furlough at the beginning of December, and we were on our own. I can tell you that if we had not been categorically assigned there, I would have felt guilty. Our assignment consisted of preaching once on Sunday and leading a Bible study Wednesday evening. The rest of our time was spent getting to know the small congregation, planting roses in the manse garden and taking small orientation trips. It was not a surprise when the Mission began to encourage us to visit other churches of our denomination both in Viña and Santiago. In fact a sort of "get to know you" tour was arranged.

It was on one such tour that we met Francisco and his wife Sonia—who would one day become the first Chilean pastors of La Cordillera Church in Santiago. At the time, I had no idea the impact our vision would have on the members of the National Church. We discovered that many thought our vision of reaching the middle and upper class was at best naïve—for some it seemed outright controversial. As I finished sharing with all the passion I still retain for that vision, at the back of the church a young couple was sitting. Francisco nudged his wife and said, "One day I will be working with that man." No truer words were spoken, although we didn't get to know each other for nearly six years.

The first two summers, I was invited to attend the National Church's summer camp, held on the farm property of missionaries just south of Temuco. While I truly enjoyed my time there, it really demonstrated to me the stark contrast between the profile of the existing National Church and the work we had been called to.

The National Church is largely a southern church, culturally as well as physically. Chile is very diverse in terms of its people. Those known as southerners do not feel comfortable in Santiago, and the Santiaguinos are thought of as cold, distant and inhospitable by those in the south. Many who live in the capital think of southerners as poor country cousins and somewhat condescendingly feel sorry for them. In keeping with those biases, camp in the south consisted of tents and outhouses: no running water and no hot water except for coffee and tea. Washing was done in the river and was also called swimming. The differences between the northern city culture and the southern rural life here at camp could not have stood in more stark juxtaposition.

I reiterate I loved my time there and made several lifelong friends. There was no wavering however, our call was to Santiago.

Ministry in Viña del Mar

Once our hearts had changed regarding our orders to go to Viña, our attitudes quickly followed. We had been ordered to work in arguably the most beautiful city on the west coast of South America. For the first few months, we lived in an apartment on the Pacific Ocean that actually had a tunnel and direct access to a magnificent sandy beach. We were assigned to do a language course that mainly consisted of doing a lot of reading. No one told us we couldn't read on the beach, and as we entered September the weather began to improve, and before Christmas we both had nice tans!

Here in our fourth floor apartment, we had our first taste of earth tremors. We had never before experienced an earthquake and had no idea what to expect. I had left Ann in bed; she was running a slight fever, and I was heading out on some chore.

I was blithely waiting for the elevator to arrive, and such was my ignorance that, when the door opened and the passengers fled out to the hall, I judged them to be all sissies. Yes I had felt the bump, but it meant nothing to me.

Ann later told me that back in our apartment, she was lying in bed when the chandelier began to sway. She thought for sure she was hallucinating. Our friends soon set us right. People in Chile respect earthquakes and what they are capable of doing, and never take them lightly. Some actually refuse to lock the main outside door for fear it will jam in a quake and they will not be able to escape

What a beautiful place. We found a beach about thirty minutes out of town and began to spend some of our time there. We walked down a sandy trail to the edge of the Pacific, found a nice smooth rock to lean against, and sat and read to the sound of the surf in the warmth of the sun. Later that spring, I took pictures of wild flowers I encountered on the path on the way down. Just on that short stroll down there were something like twenty-seven different varieties, such was the beauty of that location.

Later we began to spend our day off in Santiago. Through a mutual friend, we were re-introduced to the Jalil family. We had met them in passing on our stopover in Bolivia before arriving in Chile; they were later to be strategic in the starting of the Cordillera Church. We went once a week, by bus, to Santiago then by cab to their house, where we had lunch and prayed for the future church.

In Bible college in Regina, Saskatchewan, we had met Walter and Estella Perez, who were from Buenos Aires. We had always hoped to be able to visit them, and when another good friend,

Charlie Cook, arrived from Bolivia, we set the wheels in motion. Charlie made things easy for us as he was fluent in Spanish. A date was set and plans made.

Trip to Argentina

We had planned this trip for some time, but it was January of 1983 before we could go. We phoned our friend Walter in Buenos Aires just as soon as we knew we were able to travel. We gave him our schedule and arrival time, and he agreed to meet us. It was nearly a ruinous mistake that we did not take his phone number with us.

The bus ride from Santiago, Chile, to Mendoza, Argentina, was spectacular. The climb up from the Chilean side in order to cross the majestic Andes mountains involves traversing Los Caracoles. I am not sure how many switchbacks are involved; I only remember that, near the top, we could look down probably three or four thousand feet to where we had been some forty minutes earlier.

Then came the tunnel Conquistadores. Even at that height, some 3,175 meters (10,417 ft.) the Andes still tower over the road to their average height of 12,000 feet. Shortly after exiting the tunnel on the Argentine side having climbed to 3,500 meters during the 3,000 meter tunnel, we had a magnificent view of spectacular Mount Aconcagua, the highest mountain outside of Asia which soars to 6,962 meters (22,841 ft.). We were blown away by all we had seen and experienced that day. Thankfully we passed through customs with no complications.

We had decided to treat ourselves to ride on the "white glove special," the first-class train from Mendoza to Buenos Aires. At the ticket station we asked for three tickets and were quoted the price. We pulled out our money—US dollars—and were met with an angry glare. "We do not accept *those* dollars here." At first shocked, it then dawned on us why. How could we have been so naïve?

The war of Las Malvinas or the Falkland Island War had just ended. There was no love lost between Chile and Argentina and even less between Argentina and the USA. Chile had been seen as less than neutral and suspected of aiding and abetting the English. The Americans were seen as the enemy and thus the ire of many Argentines resulted in making life difficult wherever possible for Americans. Thus our American dollars would not be accepted.

In times of trouble, we have learned that the rest of the world draws little distinction between Canadians and Americans. Our Canadian passports did nothing to help us. We would somehow have to change some American money into Argentine pesos. As is often the case when things begin to go badly, the complications themselves cause other complications. This was clearly our position. It was Saturday, and all the banks were closed.

We were faced with finding someone on the street to exchange our US dollars. We were all apprehensive. Would we get mugged when they found out we had cash on us? Would we find an honest money changer? I don't remember how many dollars we changed between the three of us. I do remember receiving over a million Argentine pesos. So many that we felt sure it must be counterfeit. It took just long enough to find a money changer and make the exchange that we missed our train and its first-class dining room, air conditioning and compartments. We would not be leaving until early afternoon of the next day, and the only train available we christened "the cattle train."

Our first attempt to pass this money was at a hotel. Of course with the changes in plans we needed to stay the night. To our considerable relief they accepted the money. No problem. We hadn't eaten for quite some time, and now that we had time to kill, we went out to join the crowd and find a place to eat.

January is the height of summer in Argentina and, even in Mendoza, which is high in the mountains, it was nice and warm even at night. We ordered steaks, fries and salads and many ice-cold cokes until we satisfied our huge thirst. Argentine beef is world-renowned, and these steaks were delicious and huge, splaying over our plates. We dined in style at that sidewalk café and returned to our hotel renewed and content, especially when we found out that our meal had cost us less than two dollars per person. Such was the inflation in Argentina at that time.

Earlier than needs be we went to the train station the next day to purchase our tickets without incident. Then, right on time, we boarded and began the long trip across the pampas to the Atlantic coast and Buenos Aires. On this train there would be no white glove service, in fact, no service at all. Evening finally arrived and we did our best to sleep. Ann and I huddled up on one uncomfortable wooden train seat and Charlie a couple of rows behind us.

Hot? Stifling comes to mind. We lamented thinking that the train we had missed had air conditioning. Our train's air conditioning consisted of leaving windows open. The night passed, and

I think we might have slept a couple of winks except that worry is a sure cause of insomnia. We knew that we were going to be a full day late and that we were on a completely different train than originally planned. Further we knew that Walter had a commitment on this day and had no assurance he would even be there, and of course we had no phone number.

Night did pass, and I remember waking up feeling incredibly filthy and turning back to see how Charlie had fared during the night. He smiled at us, and I burst out laughing. His first words were, "Never again." We all looked like caricatures. Our faces were black from the smoke and dust of the trip. Only our teeth and eyes were white.

We arrived dirty and tired but safe and sound, thinking of our next step. How to get in touch with Walter? The main train station in Buenos Aires is huge. There are some eleven rail lines that converge there from all points of the country. Additionally the train station is located above all lines of the subway system. Here at this hub where all lines meet gather thousands of people. We stepped off the train into this moving mass.

But where should we go? We did our best to avoid being pushed along with the crowd and decided that our only option was to pray. Not an elegant prayer as I remember, more like, 'God help us please!' Yet another time in our lives God had answered before we asked. The words were not yet fully out of my mouth when I heard over my shoulder a timid voice saying "Snowsell. . . .Snowsell?"

We met our rescuer, a fellow missionary sent by Walter to find his missing friends. He told us he didn't know where to begin or what to do, but that at that same instant he also had just prayed, and God had told him to just say our name.

My memories of this trip are indelible. We were living in Viña del Mar, which I am sure didn't have 500,000 inhabitants. Santiago recorded a population of five million, but we did not yet live there nor fully appreciate what that meant. Here we were in the middle of a Buenos Aires, a city of nine million.

Walter took us on a tour to see some of the things our church denomination was doing there. We visited an area of apartment buildings—mile after mile of buildings, each one a copy of the former and each complex containing nearly three thousand people. Imagine, each building a mission field.

One day the three of us braved a trip to the centre of town on our own. One of the main streets in downtown BA is called "Los Libertadores" I can't remember if it is sixteen or eighteen lanes wide. We stood in amazement then decided we would cross. Of course we waited for the lights to change, but it turned out that was no assurance. Less than half way across we looked in the other direction to see a flock of buses, eight abreast, hurling towards us. We turned and fled back to the sidewalk shaken but laughing at ourselves nevertheless.

Walter took us out for supper, Argentine time. We left the house well after eleven. I thought that all the restaurants would be closed before we arrived and found instead that many were just opening. Very sensibly in the heat of summer they don't venture out until things begin to cool off. One in the morning is a perfect time to eat. Getting there, however, was an adventure on its own.

This restaurant was located a little ways out of town, and we had to take the freeway. I wasn't concerned at first that Walter didn't turn on more than the parking lights on the car. Surely he will turn on the lights when we leave the city. Not so. In those days the majority of Argentines thought it wise to conserve their headlights by not using them. Thus we sped down the freeway more or less in the dark being surprised from time to time as we could hear cars passing or being passed but not actually seeing them. When we finally arrived, it was after midnight. Upon entering I saw that indeed we were the only ones and that the chairs had been stacked on the tables, but instead of being late we were in fact early, and the restaurant didn't start to fill up until nearly one in the morning.

We also went another day to a restaurant called La Casa de Papas. I have returned several times over the years to this House of Potatoes and have never been disappointed. I love Argentine beef partly because it is so tasty but also because it is affordable. There is a saying in Argentina that as long as there is beef and *mate** Argentines are content. *an argentine tea

I am not sure how we got back to Chile, but I believe we flew. There had been just enough adventures.

Pastoral Experiences

About four months after our arrival in Viña, we were located in our permanent home the church's manse. It was located on top of one of the hills and was directly across the street from the president's summer residence. We often watched as the president's entourage came and went, which always involved a great deal of security and the visible presence of guns. As newcomers this was quite a cultural shock for us. This shock elevated to near panic-stricken one day as I looked out with binoculars from our upstairs bedroom window over into the compound to see what I could see. Slowly I panned what I could see of the property and began casually to look into the barracks that housed the president's body-guards. What I saw took me from mildly inquisitive to utter panic in less time than it takes to tell. As I gazed through a window I made glass to glass contact with a soldier training the sights of his high powered rifle on me. As I remember I dropped to the floor. I don't remember if I fainted.

Pastoring even a small church has its commitments, and one of the influential members of the congregation, who I will call Aunt Suzy, fell ill and was near death. The family wanted me to stay close at hand and so, reluctantly, some travel plans we had were placed on hold. Aunt Suzy had fallen out of fellowship with the church some years ago but still held great authority. I was told, "Don't visit her. She will get angry and throw you out as soon as she finds out who you are."

Good enough for me. However, one afternoon as we prepared for our siesta, I clearly heard God's voice telling me in no uncertain terms to go and visit Aunt Suzy. I argued briefly with this internal voice, thinking, *This is crazy, first of all they won't let me in*—she was at an exclusive, private clinic. *Second, even if I do get in, I will run into one of the family and they will tell me to leave. Third, what if they let me in and no family is there and Aunt Suzy is in a coma! God, do You really know what You are doing?*

I drove the twenty minutes to the private clinic with absolutely no conviction and parked the car. I trudged in only to find that there was no one at the reception desk. I am not sure how I found the room, but when I got there, I was surprised there was no one with her. Now the real surprise: Aunt Suzy was, of course, asleep, but when I entered, after just a few minutes, she woke up and turned to face me. I asked her if she knew who I was, and she replied, "Yes."

"Aunt Suzy," I asked, "are you ready to die?"

"No," she answered.

"Would you like to be?" I asked.

"Yes," she replied with tears in her eyes.

There in that room, Aunt Suzy made her peace with Jesus. Shortly she sat up, lifted her arms towards heaven, smiled and lay back down. She then entered an eternal sleep.

Nothing happens by coincidence or by chance in the believer's life. All, *absolutely all*, is being guided by a sovereign God. Such was the case in our assignment to this Scottish Presbyterian Church on the west coast of Chile.

This church turned out to be not just historic in terms of its beginnings but influential in the beginning of Protestantism in the entire country of Chile.

It is commonly accepted that Union Church was the first Protestant church built on the west coast of South America.

It is also accepted that the first non-Catholics buried in Chilean soil are interred in the cemetery located in Valparaiso, the adjoining sister-city of Viña. Prior to this time, Protestants were required to bury their dead at sea.

David Trumbell, the founder of the Union Church, is buried there. His huge black granite headstone stands on the Protestant side of the cemetery as a reminder to the change he brought as a result of his life and ministry. It was in Valparaiso that I performed my first funeral and that Aunt Suzy was finally laid to rest.

Trip to Ecuador

Taken from A Heritage of Miracles

> *When we lived in Viña, you, Colin, in particular found it hard to adjust to dorm life—so hard in fact, that early in May of 1983 the school asked Daddy to come to Quito.*

Oh how I wanted to go too! But we barely had enough money saved for one ticket. So I prayed that, if God wanted me to go too, He would send the money. Then I confidently went to the post office each day and confidently opened up each envelope, confidently waiting for the cheque which never came.

Of course the church people knew of Doug's trip to Quito, but only one person knew we were praying for money for mom: Susanna the maid. She had just accepted the Lord, and we wanted to encourage her to pray for something specific.

One day, about a week before Daddy was due to leave, we got a phone call from a dingbat in some unknown travel agency, telling us we could come and pick up our ticket. Daddy had bought his ticket through the Mission in Santiago, but this was a travel agency in Valpo. Daddy checked with the mission— no, his ticket was waiting for him in the office in Santiago. We chalked it up to the fact that this girl was a dingbat.

Meanwhile, we came to the last day for the mail before Daddy's trip. I walked down to the post office in the afternoon with Susanna. On the way we talked about Dad's trip. Susanna said she was puzzled why no one had given me the money I had asked them for.

"Oh no, Susanna," I explained, "I haven't asked anyone for money, only God. You are the only one who knows we are praying for money." I could see that she was shaken—she obviously hadn't been too concerned about praying until that moment!

That day there was not even a letter in the post box. I trusted God—it must mean that He knew it would be better for Colin that I not be there. I trusted Him to fill my days and take away my heartache.

Later that same afternoon, we went over to tea at the home of one of the church members. We had always enjoyed ourselves there, but this afternoon there were always lulls in the conversation that the hostess didn't try to fill, and I just couldn't have cared less. So dear Dad took up the slack and began babbling on and on about trivia, including the dingbat travel agent. I really was rather annoyed at Daddy's prattle and was quite relieved when it was finally time to go home.

Later that evening the phone rang, and I heard Daddy saying, "Oh, oh, I didn't know, I didn't understand." It often happened in those days that we didn't understand. I wondered what bloop had been committed. Then Daddy hung up and sat on the edge of the bed and said dazedly, "Ann, that was the _____s. That travel agent that phoned was telling us about a ticket that they had bought for YOU. They wanted it to be anonymous, and they wondered why they hadn't heard the "news." It was only at tea today that they realized we had refused to go and get the ticket. Ann, you are coming with me to Quito!"

God had provided a miracle, and we were so sure we knew how He would do it, that we nearly missed His provision! I hate to think what would have happened if we hadn't gone to tea or if Dad hadn't chit-chatted!

And, as is so very often the case, God had more than one purpose in His miracle...

When Susanna came to work the next day, I met her and told her the story and that I too would be going to Quito. As I talked, she went pale, her eyes got huge, she began to tremble and back towards the wall. When I had finished, she gasped, "God heard me! God answered my prayer! GOD heard me!" It was probably her first prayer from her heart for another human being, and God answered in spades. He did a miracle—not just for me, but for Susanna—to show her that this miraculous powerful God loves, cares, and answers prayers.

Campaign in Valdivia

As my language skills improved, I began to receive more invitations to speak in the National Church. One such invitation took me to Valdivia, a city in the south in August. To fully appreciate the circumstances, you need to remember in Chile August is the middle of winter and that going south means getting closer to the Antarctic! In Valdivia there was snow on the ground.

The church was representative of many of the National Churches of that time, especially those located in the south—small and humble. The clapboard exterior barely kept out the rain. The wind penetrated at will, and daylight was visible through the walls in several places. In the centre of the building was the only source of heat a potbelly wood stove.

The platform was at one end of the small building, but as it was nearly a matter of survival, I decided to preach from the centre, near the stove! What I spoke about and what happened must be recorded in heaven somewhere. All I remember is my accommodation and the cold.

I was billeted in one of the better houses with one of the more affluent families of the church. As with all Chileans, my hosts were gentle and generous. They did their very best to make me feel at home. We returned after the service and enjoyed *tecito* or *'los once'* [afternoon tea] in the kitchen near their wood stove.

Suspecting that the rest of the house did not have heat, I lingered there as long as possible.

The inevitable came, and I was taken to my quarters, a simple room with a bed typical of that area of Chile: a chain mattress that would be more aptly called a hammock and a nice warm thick mattress covered with an eiderdown.

I was exhausted, and it looked just great to me. I fell into bed and buried my head under the covers to get warm only to discover that I was not alone! The crawling feelings on my legs and torso made me want to leap out of bed. The intense cold forbade that option. I did my best to sleep, and in the morning counted up the many bites left by my night companions—fleas.

Oh for a shower. There were two main ways to heat water in Chile. The gas version, known as a califont, heats water on demand as it circulates through a series of coils over an open flame—this home did not have one of those. My dismay was allayed temporarily to find their shower did come with the second method of heating which was an electrical attachment located at the shower head. I tried many times to get it to work, and remember being torn between the concern that standing naked in a damp shower tinkering with an electrical attachment that had some bare wires showing would eventually kill me and the dread of cold water in that icy concrete shower stall. The water from the shower was not far from freezing—it hurt my head; gave me a headache. Suffice it to say, that was my only shower during my three day stay, and it was a brief shower at that.

At the risk of seeming negative about my friends in the National Church, I recall another story. One of our churches in Viña is located in the humblest of neighbourhoods called Viña Alta because it is way up a hill. Unlike North America, the poor suburbs are usually located up the hill most likely because of the prevalence of earthquakes. This is not merely a potential problem as it has real historic consequences. Although I digress, the main cemetery of Viña is located on one of its eleven hills. During one severe earthquake it is reported that some of the tombs opened up and caskets were seen sliding down the hill towards the main street of town.

Typically many of these poor churches have a small attached house to accommodate the pastor and his family. The purpose of my visit was to get to know the young bachelor pastor of this church.

True to form for Chileans his hospitality and willingness to share from the little that he had resulted in him inviting me to join him for breakfast—which I had actually eaten much earlier but agreed to in order to not to offend. Eggs were on the menu and that was OK with me. Not much you can do to damage eggs— or so I had thought.

He cracked several eggs into a cold frying pan into which he began to pour a generous amount of vegetable oil. I discovered later that the amount of oil was actually a compliment to me, and as he served the eggs he ensured that I received the generous portion of this lubricant poured out on my plate over the eggs. My non-appetite now progressed to the point of fighting off my gag reflex as I desperately tried to accept his generosity and to eat this near poisonous offering.

Brandon is Benched

Our son Brandon discovered a love for sports during his time in Quito, especially soccer. In fact he excelled. It was then a huge shock to him when he returned in January of 1984 for his junior year and arrived the day of tryouts to find that he was benched for the rest of the season.

Viña del Mar, where he had spent Christmas vacation, is at sea level; Quito is located at over 9,000 feet. This change combined with the fatigue of a long trip and the emotional drain of yet again saying goodbye to his family resulted in his doing poorly at the try outs which occurred the day after his return from vacation.

The coach was adamant—benched. After many weeks of riding the bench, Brandon asked to be sent back to the junior team where at least he could play. The coach cursed at him in the presence of his peers and called him derogatory names. Brandon dropped soccer altogether. So much for Christian charity at a Christian school.

It is small consolation that this coach eventually was disciplined. Incredibly he transferred to another Alliance school. It could be argued that this incident in Brandon's life influenced or caused his spiritual decline that lasted for several years. The fact this incident happened and was witnessed by many remains in my mind as a blemish on the reputation of the Christian and Missionary Alliance Church, its leaders and its staff.

Our Quito Adventures

In February of 1984, we made a trip to Ecuador to visit our boys. While we were there, we were offered the chance to go down to the jungle. The only thing that would have caused us to turn down this opportunity was if it had interfered with our time with our boys. It would not, so we enthusiastically agreed.

We were to leave very early the next morning to travel up and over the Andes and then down to the Brazilian side into the jungle near a place called *Três Rios* [Three Rivers]. The bus depot in Quito was bustling, and we strolled around in the predawn light until we found our bus. I call them jungle buses. I am not sure if the Ecuadorians called them anything in particular, but to us from North America they were small, even tiny. They probably held no more than thirty passengers and the roof was so low that we had to hunch over to walk inside.

In due time all were aboard, and we set off. Quito is 2,800 metres (about 9,186 ft.) above sea level and the trip would see us cross over the Andes at an altitude of approximately 16,000 feet. Remembering that oxygen masks deploy at 10,000 feet if an aircraft loses cabin pressure will give you some appreciation of our experience.

Forget the concept of paved roads with clearly marked centre lines and wide shoulders. There are no shoulders at all, and at times the road is not wide enough for two buses to pass. The best part of the trip was up the mountain. Best, because we were in ignorant bliss of what was to follow and because the bus couldn't gain much speed.

In fact the nearer we came to the summit, the less speed we maintained. Finally the bus lugged up the grade in its lowest gear, and we remembered that due to the lack of oxygen at this altitude, internal combustion motors lose over seventy percent of their power.

Our first stop was at a building near the top of the pass that probably was a canteen. My eyes were fixed on other things. We had probably been on the road for four hours by this time and some were in need of a bathroom break. I noticed that not many women stepped off the bus. Ann may have been one of the first. We got as far as the exit, and she began to step down only to turn quickly and flee back to her seat. The one and only bathroom was evidently located near the rear wheel of the bus and there was a line up.

That taken care of, we boarded and resumed our trip. Now we were going downhill on slopes as steep as we had just come up. As we careened down I could see from my vantage point behind the driver through the folding doors down past the edge of the road that seemed perilously close to the wheels down into what appeared to be open free fall for over 1,000 feet. On one side a steep cliff on the other side a huge abyss, and thus we continued for several hours.

On much of this trajectory we could see huge pipes, part of the oil pipe line that pumps oil from the Amazon side of the Andes over to the main Ecuadorian port of Guayaquil on the Pacific. It was an amazing engineering feat to pump oil from only a few thousand feet altitude over the Andes Mountains at some 16,000 feet, down to Guayaquil at sea level. This feat was made possible by huge pumping stations located every few hundred meters on the way up and huge de-accelerators strategically placed on the way down.

The first time I saw a bus coming towards us up the grade in front I grew tense. Could we pass? It must be possible. I don't believe the buses actually made contact but our missionary guide assured me that they often did scrape. Slowing down was not an option for either driver.

After supper that evening, at the end of our day our guide asked us, "How far do you think we have travelled?" We had been on the road for nearly six hours and had travelled only forty-five miles which will give you further appreciation for the conditions.

—

We stayed at a mission station near the village of *Três Rios*. Just as we had completed what I thought was a life-threatening epic journey over the Andes we were faced with the final lap. To arrive at the station, we had to cross a small tributary of the Amazon on a homemade bridge that was not much wider than the jeep we were now riding in. I am sure it was a swinging bridge although they assured me that the swinging was in no way dangerous. I held my breath for the thirty seconds it took to creep across.

In the jungle, walls and windows are not as important as screens. Most of the rooms in fact did not have windows, only screens. The plumbing was outside and the shower water was heated in the barrel that was sitting on top of the shower giving it all the gravitational flow it needed. Ann was terrified the first time she used the toilet as she encountered a snake. We were told not to worry about him. "He lives there and kills the poisonous bugs and beetles." We were then shown an elaborate bug collection and were told, "All these were caught in and around the house."

The next day we were invited to go on a trip down river to visit a school that was supported by the mission. Imagine! A trip down the Amazon in a dugout canoe. We drove in the jeep down to the place on the river that was a hub for river travel in that area. It was a hive of activity as the people wanting to use the services of the canoes also attracted venders. We could have had our choice of a small monkey or a young parrot for the extravagant price of half a dollar. We did settle for three Auca spears on the return trip—the Auca are one of the indigenous people of that region. The spears were an interesting item to get onto the plane for the return trip to Chile.

Our missionary guide did all the bargaining with the boatmen, and they arrived at a price. We all climbed into the long narrow craft and started down river. The Napo is a tributary of the Amazon River and one can follow 4,000 miles of navigable waters all the way to the Atlantic. Even there in Ecuador it was already a sizeable river that would be dangerous to ford even without the crocodiles and piranhas.

We glided smoothly with the current, fascinated with an entirely new panorama to our eyes—a jungle. The trees for the most part hid any shore and in some places were a danger to unsuspecting or inexperienced boaters who could be knocked out of the canoe by an outstretched branch. Travel other than the river would be all but impossible because of the densest vegetation we had ever seen. With good reason, the river is called the highway of the jungle.

After perhaps a forty-five minute ride we reached our destination. The boatman carefully maneuvered his craft around into the current and we snuggled into a small man-made landing area. This then led to a steep climb up to a small plateau that had been cleared and on which the school buildings were located.

Our arrival signalled school was out. Visitors are rare this far into the jungle, and white visitors even rarer. We were in fact strange enough that just about everyone wanted to have their picture taken with us—even the teachers. By-and-by one of the teachers asked if we would join them for a cup of *chicha*. The word conjured up for me the idea of Chilean chicha which is new, still-fermenting wine. For reasons of decorum I glanced at our missionary guide and he confirmed with a glance that this was their way of honouring us and that it would be an insult to refuse as they were favouring us by offering. We said yes.

Picture-taking and excited banter continued for a time between the children who spoke in their own language as they knew little or no Spanish. Then I noticed one of the teachers coming out of one of the several small buildings carrying what for the world looked like a kidney-shaped stainless steel bedpan.

Horror. I had expected a glass or perhaps a cup of reddish looking new wine. This lack of understanding was of course caused by my near total ignorance of jungles. Thinking back obviously there are no grapes. I was all too soon to discover what jungle chicha was.

In the jungle there is no refrigeration and things decompose very quickly. Also there is no water purification and so this one process of fermentation serves to purify and to prevent spoiling of juices. Soon the bedpan came close enough to see that it contained a liberal amount of white, chalky, slimy liquid—jungle chicha. Chicha is made here out of the root of the yucca or jungle potato. It is chewed up and then spit into large containers and left to ferment. I am not sure how long this vintage had been brewing, but it certainly wasn't going to be awarded a gold label.

I glanced once more at our guide and was given the sign to drink up. As I accepted the stainless steel container and gazed into it I began to pray, *Oh God, I believe that for the sake of these people I should drink some of this, and as my duty to You, I will attempt to do so. May I at this time remind You that it will be Your responsibility to help me not to vomit.* This practical prayer completed I took the container to my lips and took a deep draught. It was more horrible than I had imagined. Together with the milky appearance was a slimy texture that included bits of substance; it felt and looked altogether like—and pardon the vernacular—snot.

After a short time of farewells we wended our way back towards the canoe. I noticed that I was unmistakably feeling the effects of that brew. It had quite a kick. The next day we returned to Quito, very grateful to have had this once in a life time opportunity to have visited a primitive area of a remote jungle base.

While in Quito, the dorm parents encouraged us to get away for a time alone with our boys. A small place several kilometres out of town with individual cabins was suggested. We were driven there and told how to get back to Quito by bus.

I think the time there was OK. It was filled with tension, sadness and the certainty that it was not a possible solution to have the boys return with us to Chile. It did give us time to listen and hug them as they poured out their young hearts to us.

The boys have learned to refer to difficulties we experience together as a family as "adventures." Several times we have heard them ask, "Are we having another adventure?"

The day came for our return to Quito, and an adventure did begin. No one had remembered that that day was a national holiday. No buses were running. Further, the locals, mainly Quechewa Indians, had taken advantage the night before to really tie one on. As we walked out to the main road we saw them sleeping it off in the ditches. There is a type of loyalty between husband and wife at these times we were told. They evidently take turns in their drinking binges so that one can stand guard while the other drinks into happy oblivion. Now one stood guard as the other slept it off.

At the highway it became apparent what was happening, and it slowly dawned on us as no buses either came or went that, in all likelihood, there would be none. Now the dilemma: Our reservation had ended at the cabin and even if it hadn't we had run out of money. We had no alternative but to head back to Quito. Shortly after we began to walk carrying our bags a remarkable car came careening down the road. Remarkable because in South America, American cars are not often seen and one as large as this boat really stood out.

They stopped after passing us and began to back up. "Where are you going? There are no buses today. Why don't you jump in?"

Thank you, God. They claimed to be relatives of some kind to the president and were very kind. They probably would have driven us straight to the dorm if it weren't for the fact the car overheated due to a leak in the radiator. We were now within hiking distance and set off with much lighter hearts.

Planting a Forest

If pressed to answer what we did as missionaries, I answer that we were church planters, although I am not sure to this day what that means. One of my mentors used to encourage us by asking, "Do you know how to plant a forest?" The question demands a negative response. However, when it is rephrased as a series of questions starting with, "Do you know how to dig a hole? Can you put a tree in that hole?" You realize that you could, given enough time, plant a forest.

Such is the task of church planting. Can you lead someone to saving faith in Christ? Can you disciple that person in the basics of their new faith? Then given enough time you can plant a church. A significant difference and departure from past methods was that we chose to live within the community in which we planned to start a church. Heretofore nearly all work had been done from a central mission location.

The difference between reforestation and the church is that church planting can only be done in the power and strength of the Holy Spirit and following closely or walking closely with Christ who is the head of the church.

That was what occurred in Chile. We did lead and teach a number of people Christian basics, but our complete ignorance of the task at hand can only be appreciated in retrospect. God, in His mercy, was able to make up for our deficiencies in many ways and on many occasions.

Our preparation began before we arrived in Chile and included stopping in La Paz, Bolivia, to visit our very good friend Charlie, who was doing missionary work there. While in La Paz we accompanied him on Sunday to the church he was attending. There we met Mario and Ofelia Jalil. We thought nothing more of Mario and Ofelia until Charlie came to visit us in Chile some months later.

One day during his stay he said, "Do you remember that family you met in La Paz? Well they have moved to Santiago, and I would like you to meet them." As good as his word we went with him to Santiago and met the entire Jalil family and found out that Mario was the head of the Food and Agriculture Organization (FAO) of the United Nations in Latin America.

They lived on the 11th floor of an apartment in Santiago. Which is to say that their apartment occupied the entire 11th floor with balconies on all sides. This location would prove to be strategic for us.

In what seemed to be a short time, our posting in Viña ended. I guess that is a tribute to how much God can change a heart that tries its best to keep Him in first place. As reluctantly as we had arrived in Viña eighteen months earlier, now we found it very difficult to leave all these friends in order to respond to our primary call to Santiago. Very fortunately many of those dear people are still close friends and still come into our lives from time to time.

Santiago 1984–1985

Our First House: Vitacura

We arrived in the capital to begin what we soon began to see as mission impossible—to find a house in the target area of our city. The Mission wisely has caps on such things as rent, food, mileage etc. These amounts were all established thinking only of working in certain parts of Santiago and not in the upper class areas.

We were encouraged not to work in Las Condes of Santiago. We were still the newbies, highly acclaimed perhaps, but we had made no names for ourselves. We were given many reasons not to consider Las Condes: very expensive; thought to be unresponsive; no precedents etc.

Truth be told our first real obstacle came from the mission itself: Yes, we *could* work in this area although the mission thought it ill-advised, and, as such, we would not receive any special compensation and would have to find a house for the same rates as all the other missionaries.

The fact we might not find a home within the price range seemed likely. In fact after several weeks it seemed *almost* a foregone conclusion.

Taken from *A Heritage of Miracles*

It seems God loves to provide homes in miraculous ways. You were in Quito when we were house hunting in Santiago. This would have been November of 1984. It was summer and sweltering, which only added to our discouragement. We knew we wanted to live in Las Condes, so Granny and I made a list of all the homes listed in our price range that had three bedrooms, a phone, and a utility room. With great confidence we set out. We weren't disappointed that the first place was a dump, but at the end of the day we were sticky, hot, and not too happy. The next day, all fresh and eager again, we went with Mrs. Barker and Mrs. Koskela, and found even dumpier places. We did find one lovely home, but it had already been rented. It was far south too—still in Las Condes, but close to Nuñoa.

During this time, Daddy was south of Temuco at a family camp. In the remaining days before he came back, we continued to plod along, mom and I, Doris and I—but for the amount of money we were allowed for rent, there was nothing in Las Condes.

Then home came Daddy! All refreshed and exuberant and ready to go. He scoffed at our dejection and boldly set out. The first thing he did was to have Ofelia phone her real estate lady to begin looking for us. The lady was thrilled to help a friend of Ofelia's but when she realized that we weren't as rich as Ofelia, she sent a part-time girl to us: we never did see Ofelia's friend!

This girl phoned us the next day, and Daddy, Granny and I set out excitedly to find our house!

However, we only found more dumps! Except that this time we had been driven there. Big deal!

We began to think that perhaps we should be looking at an apartment rather than a house, and began scanning the newspaper for these. Did you know that there are very few three bedroom apartments with telephones in Santiago? We began to feel desperate.

Then we read of an apartment in Vitacura, so Daddy, Granny and I set off again. On a map, Vitacura looks far away, so we hadn't looked there before, but as we drove there I realized that it wasn't really all that far and that it was a beautiful area. And the apartment! I loved it! But Daddy didn't, and I couldn't persuade him to change his mind. He wouldn't budge! (And am I ever glad he wouldn't!) So we kept on looking, although by this time we pretty well knew that what we were looking for in our price range was impossibility. We kept on plugging away because we couldn't believe that God would let us down.

The end of the month was the next weekend and everyone told us to be sure to look then, because if ever there was going to be a house, it could be then.

But we had a dilemma! We had been invited to a wedding that weekend in Viña. Anderly's son, Michael, was getting married, and you know how much we love Anderly. Besides, we had looked forward to going back for a visit while Granny was still here and we had said yes long before we had any idea that we would be house hunting. What to do? You know the rule we have: God is sovereign, and is well able to bring things to us in whatever order He chooses.

Therefore, whatever He brings first is what He wants us to do.

So, then we knew that, even though it looked crazy, God wanted us to go to Viña. So we continued with our original plans. We were considered crazy by all the experienced house hunters, but we stuck to our convictions that God is sovereign.

So off we went to Viña. We had a super time at the wedding, the church, and especially visiting our old neighbours, Sergio and Jimena. We spent a couple of hours with them one afternoon, and as we visited, we recounted all the frustrations of finding a non-existent house. Sergio was in an expansive mood, and right then and there picked up the phone and called long distance to his friend in Santiago. He said, "Enrique, my good friend needs a house and needs a very nice one." Enrique said, "Anything for a friend." And we left it at that.

When we got back to Santiago, Doug and Enrique got together, and Enrique showed him a house. HOUSE! It was more like a mansion! Doug gulped and tried to explain that this house was too nice.

That was Monday. On Tuesday we made the decision to look for a house that we needed, and not to bother about the price. We remembered the Old Testament story of the Israelite nation crossing the Jordan. The waters didn't part until the priests put their feet in, not before. We believed that if we found the right house, that God would supply the extra money.

We started again! I phoned a lady I had met and she whizzed over and whizzed us to see two houses and whizzed away and we never say her again. What a dingbat! Still undaunted, Doug went out on his own in the dead heat of the afternoon to see some others. He came home thoroughly discouraged and dejected. For the first time, I was worried—I always am if Daddy gets down.

So there we sat—in a borrowed home with only a few weeks left. The phone rang. It was Enrique. "Come right now," he said. "I've found your house." Dad felt like saying, "Oh sure you have—forget it!" but instead he agreed, and off we went. Poor Granny was too exhausted to even care—she had seen us disappointed enough times already.

With map in hand, we set out. We soon found ourselves in lovely Vitacura and turned off into a shady tree-lined street. We were driving slowly looking at the house numbers, and we came up to an abandoned house. We both groaned! "Not again!" Daddy was angry. Suddenly I saw the house number: "Doug, that's not it, it's the next one!' And we drove up to a beautiful little home with a manicured lawn. You know the one—it was your home!

The price they were asking was more than what we were allowed, but Enrique calmly and professionally ignored their asking price and offered them our price. They accepted immediately. It was January 1984, the waters had parted and we had gone through!

A miracle—obeying God, obeying His principles in spite of what circumstances indicate or what people say, and watching God provide His very best.

*At any point we could have signed for a dump—
but why settle for a dump when God has something
perfect in store? Always trust Him for a miracle.*

Bible Study at Ofelia's

We moved into our new home over a weekend. Monday we had a surprise visit from Ofelia Jalil. She came with the required house-warming gift and an invitation. Would we like to come over to her house on Thursday morning for coffee? We facetiously searched our day-timers to see if we could fit her in and found we did not have a thing to do Thursday—or for that matter any other day—and accepted the invitation.

Thursday we arrived to what had been the Polish embassy, before Pinochet seized power in 1973: a magnificent house with grand gardens. We were ushered into a large living room to discover we were not the only ones invited for coffee. Judith, Maria Mercedes and a couple of others were already there.

Coffee appeared promptly served by Ofelia with the help of their maid. Just as soon as we settled in, Ofelia asked me "Pastor would you like to share the Word with us?" This is evangelical talk for *would you give us a devotional from the Bible.*

Now I was taken aback. We had come for coffee. I hadn't even brought my Bible. Ofelia said that was not a problem and soon appeared with Bibles for everyone. Once again, as I have found to be true time after time, God had already prepared the way. Although most mornings I do spend time reading the Bible that particular morning God had impressed in my mind three points as in a sermon. I remembered them vividly and so commenced to share my spiritual breakfast with the ladies.

Once done there was a unanimous request. *Can we do this every Thursday?* Could we! This is how the impossible is done. Following a God of miracles and expecting Him to deliver according to His will and His word. Thus began our first Bible study.

Sergio and Ingrid

Sometime earlier, at a wedding, we had met a young couple by the names of Sergio and Ingrid. They lived in La Reina, an adjacent suburb to Las Condes. Sergio particularly had expressed an interest in our vision, and I decided to give him a try. In order to test his sincerity I invited him to pray with me once a week at six in the morning. First, I must repent of my doubting action. I had no right to test him that way. Second, to my utter amazement, he agreed. Getting up to pray at six is unheard of in Chile. Getting up at six am is unheard of period!

After a couple of prayer times I discovered that perhaps Sergio was testing me and that he and Ingrid already had a Bible study in Las Condes. Voila miraculously two Bible studies being held with the people we had been sent to minister to.

We were ecstatic. The mission remained skeptical.

God Directs us through Walter

One week during this time, our friend Walter came to visit us on the way back to Buenos Aires at the end of one of his evangelistic campaigns. I have always held Walter in high regard—awe really. I felt for the first time perhaps I could impress him with what we—or rather what *God* was doing.

I remember strutting my stuff before him. "Walter, we have two studies with nearly twenty-five people and we haven't even been here a full year yet. What do you think of that?"

"Dougie," he said, "it is not enough. People will come and study the Bible with you with no real commitment. You need to start a church."

I was hurt, bordering on angry. These were not the encouraging words of a friend. I paraded all the logical reasons I had why not to start a church. We didn't have a permanent location. We had no musicians and no musical instruments, nor hymn books. All these I envisioned then as being basic for a church. Then I sprung my trump card on him. "Walter," I said, "we have to return to Canada in six months for our furlough year. This is clearly not the right time to start a church. We will leave the Bible studies in the care of others, and when we return we will begin the church."

Walter did not budge one inch. "Dougie you are wrong. Start a church."

I retired to bed quite dismayed.

Before Walter got up the next morning I was having my morning devotions, and believe you me, God had been waiting for me. He gently chided me. *Doug I have gone to a great deal of trouble to send you a choice servant of mine with my instructions, and Doug, you are not listening.*

At breakfast I said, "Walter I don't know how to do this, and it scares me a lot, but we will do our best to start the church now."

The next Thursday we arrived at our Bible study, and I was very unsure of myself. How would I tell these ladies that we were going to start a church? They would think I was nuts. I left the notice until the last minute. We had our study and were just finishing our coffee after when I said hesitantly, "I think God wants us to start a church."

I was not sure my ears were hearing correctly because they all answered at the same time. "What took you so long to decide, pastor?"

And so, yet again, we ventured into the impossible. Before we left that morning we began to deal with some of the obvious needs. Where would we meet?

If we had been starting a church within the parameters of the existing National Church, perhaps we could have afforded a building or locale. It was said at the time, if you wanted to find one of our National Churches you took a bus to the end of the line; then you walked along the narrowest road until it turned into a path. The church building was sure to be nearby. On the other hand, the people of Las Condes were accustomed to considerable comforts. Where indeed to start? We brainstormed: perhaps a tent campaign. We could rent something. It was then I was taught a lesson by a sovereign God that I have never forgotten. Into my mind came a question raised by God Himself. *Doug, why do you always think of what you can afford and not what you need? Am I not the King of Kings? Are you not then a prince?*

I began to put these thoughts into words. "Perhaps God wants us to think not of what we can afford but rather what would be best. Quickly that thought became concrete. The best in Santiago at that time was the four-star Sheraton Hotel. Before we began to doubt ourselves Ofelia, Judith and I were commissioned to go to the hotel the next day to see if indeed we could get a room.

The Cordillera Church

Taken from *A Heritage of Miracles*

We knew when God called us to begin the Cordillera Church for the middle and upper classes that we would have many prejudices to break concerning evangelical churches here in Chile. This Catholic country thinks of evangelicals as poor, and their churches as poor and grubby and out of the way. So, to begin to break this mold, we needed to find a place to rent that was visible, accessible, well-known, and well-respected. We let our imaginations rove the streets of Las Condes and finally came to—THE HOTEL SHERATON! We were immediately advised by many not to even bother asking because they knew the going rate was US$200 per day. But God is a God of miracles, right? And there's absolutely no point in saying that if a person isn't prepared to act upon that belief. The worst thing anyone can do to a request is say NO, and God's Word tells us that "You have not because you ask not." So we asked!

Daddy and Ofelia went. Daddy said he has never before seen such traffic nor such confusion on the roads. They both sensed the presence of the enemy. On one street a car came straight for them at full speed! They had to pull off to avoid a head-on collision, and as they driver whizzed by, they were startled to see his glazed hate-filled eyes. They prayed God's protection, and then carried on.

When they arrived, they were received immediately by the manager, without even having to wait or to give a long explanation to his secretary.

After introductions, Daddy stated their purpose for being there and what they would need. The manager responded amiably, "Why yes! We have just the thing you need—and it will only cost US$200 per day!" Daddy began to say thank you at the same time he began to stand up, but the manager continued, "However, I can see that you can't afford that, so we'll give it to you for nothing." NOTHING! The manager then added that he would provide coffee after each meeting, and bill us for that. Well, US$20 is a lot more manageable than US$200.

Learning from Walter

I still can't believe how fortunate I was to have had the opportunity to live in the Latin culture and to have been accepted and embraced by Latinos. I say Latinos, not just Chileans, because God gave us favour with nationals in many countries.

I went to South America believing that I could impart to these poor unfortunate third world folks some wisdom that would improve their lives. Apart from the one universal truth, that it is Jesus alone that can ultimately change lives for the good, I see now that it was I who needed enlightening.

This education came in many ways. On one of Walter's visits I remember worrying about getting him to the airport on time for his departure flight back to Buenos Aires. Walter, as usual, wasn't worried at all and, in fact, decided that he wanted to stop and wander up Cerro Santa Lucia which is a well-known tourist site in Santiago, a hill with a great view of the city and the location of the first Spanish settlement.

I know I didn't enjoy the outing very much, continually glancing down at my watch. Finally Walter agreed to leave. "Dougie you worry too much."

Down the hill we went back to the car. What car? It was gone. It had only been parked about twenty minutes, but there was no sign of it. Some kind person came up and told us it had been towed for illegal parking.

Can you imagine? Walter's suitcase containing his passport and tickets were in the trunk of the car! The plane was due to leave in less than two hours; the airport was a half hour drive, if we didn't get held up by traffic, and we had no car.

I believe that I have never perspired that much before. Walter was as cool as a cucumber. We took a cab and found out where the compound was where they towed cars. We arrived before they had had time to park it and paid a fine. Believe me when I say we sped out to the airport. Walter strode into the airport unruffled and cool with probably no more than fifteen minutes to spare before the departure.

Time, or rather the way we see and use time in North America, is often a great enemy of life.

Walter has an ability to communicate great truths in very effective ways. Perhaps he acquired this ability on the way to achieving one of his three doctorates—one from Oxford. Before I repeat the lesson he taught, me let me set the background scene.

I first met Walter in 1978 in a crash summer Greek class during my time at Canadian Bible School/Canadian Theological Seminary in Regina, Saskatchewan. We had all heard of the South American student who was coming to go to the seminary. I was disappointed when the short dark-skinned South American turned out to be a very white, blond curly-haired, blue-eyed person who did not stand out from the rest of us at all.

Yet the North American mentality is pervasive. Walter would hear things like, "I bet you don't have shopping malls like this in South America?" To which Walter would simply say, "No we don't."

On our first trip to Buenos Aires, Walter took us to a Jumbo, which is a gargantuan grocery store. In Buenos Aires, large takes on a completely different meaning. We are comparing large in Regina, Saskatchewan—with its 140,000 residents—to large in Buenos Aires where over nine million lived at the time. This Jumbo store is really a huge mall under the guise of a grocery store. The staff of Jumbo drive around in golf carts! Standing at one end of the row of checkouts you would have to have field glasses to recognize a person at the 62nd one at the other side of the store; and the store is significantly longer than it is wide!

Walter, seemingly out of the blue, commented "Dougie, you really don't have anything like this in Regina." Then we howled laughing as I realized Walter had just slightly chastised my arrogant North American mindset. How I love that man.

First Service

For our first meeting of the Cordillera Church, held November of 1984 in the Sheraton Hotel, I arrived very early. I wanted to be sure everything was ready for this historic occasion. When we entered, we were told there was a problem by one of the staff. Oh me of little faith, I thought, *I knew it was too good to be true.*

He went on to say, "You are having a coffee break after the meeting?"

"Yes," I replied waiting for the bombshell I expected to fall at any moment.

"I thought so," he said. "We do have a problem. I don't see how we are going to transition between the service in one room and a different set up for the coffee break. Why don't we get you a second room for the coffee?"

In my wildest dreams I never expected that the hotel would offer us a second room at the ridiculous price we were paying. They did and it resolved another problem regarding what we were going to do with the children during the regular service—now we could have a Sunday school!

My lesson in never underestimating God continued after the first service. We transitioned to the second room after being dismissed. I believe there were twenty-five people in attendance at the first meeting. What awaited us there brought me to tears. In one corner there was a large sterling silver tureen of coffee. Then my eyes beheld the three maître d's dressed in tuxes. Two were offering fresh cookies and baked goods served on sterling silver platters; the other attending the coffee tureen. The word of God, who is the King of Kings, came again to me: *Doug never again think of yourself as poor. You are a prince, My son.*

The Cordillera church was born. Jeannette, one of Ofelia's daughters, created the logo that is still used for the church. She actually produced it in the form of a pulpit cover, which I still have in my possession.

Bombs in the Night in Santiago

We never felt at risk during our time in Santiago although these were days of violent tension between the forces of communism and Pinochet's military dictatorship. Many were the people back home who asked us when we were going to get out of the country for safety reasons. I do remember some nights counting the number of explosions. Then the next day we would read the paper only to find nothing had been reported. In time we would discover that this bridge or that building had been the target, but it was all sort of surreal. There was a definite contradiction because, at the same time, we could wander the streets of Santiago even late at night and know we were completely safe. Crime was not tolerated by the regime. Thieves were punished.

Another common sign of the severe agitation in the country was the train ride to the south. The tracks leaving Santiago passed through some marginal areas of the city, and at night the conductors would always come through before passing through these parts to securely close the blinds and douse the lights. The train was a more difficult target for the rock throwers if there were no lights.

God's Car—Another Car Story

In my first book I recounted several car miracles. These God interventions continued in Chile. An example of the different mentalities was demonstrated when we first began to look for a car. The mission encouraged us to purchase a Citroenetta which is a Volkswagen-beetle-sized Citroen only *less* luxurious. They encouraged us not to be extravagant so as to not be an affront to the National church. In my eyes, plainly said the car was ugly and surely would be an obstacle to reach the folks in our part of town. Instead this is what we did.

Taken from *A Heritage of Miracles*

When I look back and see all the miracles that God has done for that 1980 Ford Corcel in Chile, I know it was indeed God's car.

Just after we arrived in Chile, the peso started to go haywire and the prices hadn't changed—it was the ideal time to buy a car! We had a work special, but it still didn't have enough for the purchase, so we phoned a very dear and special friend and he lent us what we needed. We bought our car—you know it well. We made arrangements that all money received would be sent directly to him. However, as time went on, we became concerned that he wasn't being paid back as quickly as he should and we began to doubt our wisdom in getting the car, because it was distressing to us to owe money and especially risk the friendship of one so beloved. So, we set a deadline, and promised God to sell the car and return the money if our friend had not been paid back in full by that time.

The months went by and little by little bit the money came in. However, in the last month, we still owed $2,000. At the end of April the money hadn't come in, and we began to make preparations to sell. The following month we still had our car and we got a notice from head office about one last contribution to our car special. Can you guess for how much? $2,000—and anonymous. Can you guess when it was made? The last day of April! God's car was paid for!

It wasn't a new car, and from time to time it needed repairs. One time, while still in Viña, there was a bill coming due, and we had no money to pay it. That day in the mail we received a letter from a man who had never written us before, nor has written us since. Inside the envelope was a cheque in Canadian dollars, which, when translated to US dollars, and then to pesos, was exactly the amount of the bill! Before we even knew of this upcoming expense, God was sending us the money we would need. Remember that, boys! Our miracle-working God promises that "before you ask I will answer." And if He's so committed to a car, can you imagine how committed He is to you?

The next series of miracles are some I really can't explain because I'm not a mechanic. But I do know that I was most frustrated and annoyed at the apparently endless and always expensive repairs that happened to the car in the two weeks before Daddy, Granny and I were to go south. We were trying valiantly to save a few dollars, yet each time something happened and away would go the money, and up would go my anger level, until one day I realized that a pattern was repeating itself. I can't remember the details (I think it was the fan belt, brakes, fuel pump, and other things) but each time, when the various mechanics explained the problem and then discovered that in the near future we were planning a long trip, they said, "It's a good thing this happened now! If it had happened on the highway, while driving at highway speeds, you would probably have been killed or most certainly have been in a serious accident." I began to see that God was getting His car ready to transport safely three of His children. Instead of annoying and frustrating setbacks, I finally saw a loving God putting His protective hand over his property. Now maybe that's the biggest miracle of all—a changed heart! A changed attitude toward what appears to be lousy circumstances interfering with one's plans for enjoyment. God's protection was indeed miraculous, so too was His dealing with me.

By the way, the trip was great! God's dear car doubled its mileage with nary a hitch! I suppose the fact that it's God's car makes it obvious that the enemy would try to destroy it one way or another—if not in a breakdown or an accident, then ...

Terrorists

My ultimate joy is to introduce people to my friend Jesus Christ or to help new believers get to know Him better. I had a regular meeting with a young man who was an engineering student at the University of Chile in Santiago. We regularly met Monday mornings. Usually we met in an empty classroom, but this particular morning my friend Horacio seemed agitated and asked if we could meet out in the car because he didn't want to be interrupted.

He began to recount his weekend and his relationship with his girlfriend and how he thought he would have to end this relationship—he was an emotional mess. I listened and then offered to pray with him. We had just begun to pray when at both our windows simultaneously we heard, tap tap tap. As I began to roll down my window I smiled and said, "Horacio you got me." I believed these two young good-looking men were his friends pulling a prank on me.

However it was far from a prank.

"Please get out of the car," one of them said politely. "We are taking it."

I knew it was not a joke because they both held revolvers pointed at us. They helped us open the doors, and we got out. Then Horacio did either a very courageous or a most stupid thing; he said, "I need to get my lecture notes out of the back seat; they are my life."

As he did so he grabbed my jacket which contained all my documentation. I shudder to think what the terrorists might have done with my identification.

Yes, they were terrorists. I was shocked at their professional calmness as they stepped into my car which was parallel parked; slowly eased it out of the parking place and moved towards the first corner where they stopped, signalled and turned out of sight.

Horacio and I ran frantically with no semblance of calm to the nearest police station to report the robbery. There we were told that there had already been five cars stolen that morning. The terrorists use these cars for one of two things. They either use them to do a raid on the house of an important political person—driving by, strafing the building, then burn the car to destroy the evidence; or they fill them with explosives and leave them outside a key location such as a police station. Either way, for the owner of the vehicle, burned up or blown up, there is not much hope.

The police took the details. Horacio returned to school, and I continued my day using taxis and the bus. That same morning I had a prayer time scheduled with one of the pastors of our denomination. I had phoned Ann to assure her that I was all right, but I would soon be anything but fine. While at Victor's house the police arrived. At first I was impressed at their efficiency. They invited me to accompany them, but the look on Victor's face told me all was not well. It turns out these were the secret police, and they were not there to help me.

I was escorted to their car and seated in the back seat between two soldiers. I noticed that all four officials had automatic weapons. We drove in silence, finally turning into a lane where we were stopped in front of a huge metal gate, twenty feet high and thirty wide. The gate opened before us, and we passed through into a courtyard. By now I was not at all calm or comfortable.

I was escorted into the building, with two officers behind and two in front of me. To this day I am not sure where I was, except it looked like a special prison. We marched into this building and the smells of humanity gagged me. I could see, at the end of the corridor, we were walking towards cells and prisoners. I thought, *Well at least Pastor Victor knows what has happened to me.*

Just a few feet before we would have been on cell row, we turned, and I was asked to sit in a small cubical of an office with a table and chair. I was made to wait for some time, then an officer came and asked me to write down what had happened. I began to explain to him that I had already done this at the police station, but his reaction to my statement said I better just do it.

After an hour in this atmosphere of stench and tension, he came back and asked me to follow him. This time we began to go downstairs. I could see that we were several stories below street level when we stopped. It was another office of some kind with a desk and chair. Again the request to give a written statement.

When I finished, the paper was collected, and I was left to sit and ponder before being shown into another area on the same level where I was shown a number of books of mugshots. I didn't recognize anyone, and finally I was asked to follow them yet again. This time I was shown to an exit from the building to the street and summarily dismissed.

I had entered the prison mid-morning. It was now late afternoon. I had been confined for most of the day, and I was hungry, thirsty and very afraid. Fortunately I had enough money to pay for a cab home.

After looking into the barrel of a gun pointed with intent at your head—not to mention being taken by force into an interrogation centre by police who have the authority to never let you go—many things are never the same. I began to hear things on our telephone. I would pick up the phone and hear what sounded like room noises. I was concerned enough to mention what had happened to a new friend of mine, the Canadian Ambassador. We met nearly every month for coffee and a chat, and when I informed him of the events we came up with a strategy.

"Doug," he said, "go home and call this number. It is my private number here in the embassy and tell me what you have just told me about." Immediately upon returning home I called.

"Doug," he said over the phone, "this is serious. You will call me every twenty-four hours from now on, and if I don't hear from you, I will make some very direct and informed calls to the Chilean government."

It may be coincidence, but the noises on our telephone stopped shortly after that call.

After our car had been taken—and because of our faith—we were confident that the car would quickly be found. We carefully looked at each grey Ford Corcel we saw—we hadn't realized how many there were in Santiago! However, as time went on, and the only stolen cars found were those that the terrorists used as car bombs, our faith began to dwindle. We began to think about what other kind of car we would want, but we never thought too seriously. Whoever heard of missionaries being granted a two-car special in one term! For the record, car insurance is not common in Chile, and we had none.

On Christmas day, we were invited out for lunch, and when we came home, the phone was ringing. It was Maria Mercedes calling Ann. "Anita! They've found your car! It's listed in the paper!" She gave us the address, and as the boys were home for the Christmas holiday off the four of us went in search of our car. The police station directed us to their car lot on the other side of town, and off we went again. When we got there, an armed guard let me in to see the car. It was really rather incredible that they would let me in without a single document. I guess anything goes on Christmas day. There was our car! At first I was pretty shocked by its appearance. All the inside was covered in a fine white powder (looking for fingerprints), but the fellow pointed out some of the other cars—cars that had no wheels, no motor, no seats—and we realized that indeed we were very lucky.

The next day we hired a tow truck to take the car out and over to a garage. Within a short time we had a like-new car—God looks after His property!

As the repairs progressed, we began to see just how miraculously God had protected His car.

The terrorists had put less than fifty kilometres on it before the brand-new fan belt broke and the recently installed water pump failed! We had prayed that God would not allow His car to be used as a car bomb nor in a raid on a police station—ours had apparently been taken for the latter purpose—but when it broke down they looked inside, saw the problem, slammed the hood down and pounded it hard (the dent remained). They left it abandoned right there on the street.

As far as we were concerned, the case was closed. However, God wanted to show us in still another way how miraculous was the return of His car!

A few weeks later I received a phone call from some bureaucrat, saying there were papers for me to sign in regards to the robbery. I went and a rude little man told me to come back with two people who could vouch as to who I was. A day or two later I did so, and the petty fellow kept us waiting over two hours while he talked to a woman who I supposed was his wife. Still I did not get the papers to sign.

After that, I was summoned again to do something else, but every time this fellow stalled me. Finally I just quit trying—after all we had the car and it was this petty fellow who wanted the paper signed, not me.

Months passed and finally a young man arrived at our house with a subpoena inviting me to attend a meeting with this bureaucrat. So down I went, and the guy looked at me with exasperation and said, "Mr. Snowsell did you like your car?"

"Yes."

"Was it a nice car?

"Yes."

"Don't you *want* your car back?"

"I have my car," I said.

"How? When?" He was clearly flustered.

"Since Christmas day," I said. "I went down and towed it away."

The man was crestfallen. "You needed to sign this paper, but it doesn't matter now. You can go."

Only then did we realize that the man was waiting for a bribe. He kept stalling, thinking that I would be so desperate to get my car I would pay this corrupt official to speed up the process. God knew, so He provided a miracle of protection from even bribery, and I received our car back with no official authorization and towed it away from a police compound, on Christmas day. I call that a miracle.

Earthquake of 1985

We had our first earthquake experience shortly after we arrived in Chile and before we moved to Santiago. In comparison to the quake of 1985 it was a mere tremor. The Spanish have four different words for earthquake. Each corresponding to ratings on the Richter Scale: *Temblor* 1–3, *Terremoto* 4–6, *Sismo* 7–9 and *Cataclysmo* 10–12.

On the evening March 3, we were attending a church in downtown Santiago. People say you can hear a quake before you feel it, and perhaps that is why the dogs began to bark before we felt the movement. The earthquake began with a noise like that of a train coming in the distance, barely audible at first then becoming a roar as it passes. The sound increased, and the earth began to move, almost imperceptibly at first, and then to shake viciously.

The building we were in was made of brick, and I remember sitting there as my senses slowly filled to overload. First I heard the train, then it felt as if it was about to pass by the row in front of us. Then I watched, fascinated, as one corner of the building begin to open and shut alternately letting in light and then closing again. *Funny*, I thought, *bricks should not move like that.* Then I realized that we were all being covered with dust and that the pastor on the platform was fending off falling debris.

I am sure it all didn't last two minutes. It seemed like hours. Finally with the building still full of dust and showing the effects of having been brutally shaken, the pastor announced calmly, "I think we should all move out to the street."

There, standing amongst the rubble, together with many shaken neighbours we sang, prayed and finished the service. No one had been hurt although we had experienced a 7.8 quake that had lasted an unheard of minute and forty seconds.

All across town we could hear sirens. Fires had started, and smoke was rising from all directions. We left quickly to return to our house to inspect the damage. Shortly after we parked the car in the driveway, a strong aftershock occurred. I watched the electric wires straining on the concrete lamp posts as they flexed and relaxed. Our car stood in the drive bucking.

Why Cordillera?

How much is in a name? We could have called our church "First Church of Las Condes," "Eighth of Santiago," etc. From the first meeting, where we discussed starting the church, God guided us in naming the church. We had struggled and talked for some days about what the name should be. One day we gathered together just to pray, and it was then that God revealed both the name and the logo that have, to this day, branded Cordillera as a strong, stable, visible church. All are characteristics of the majestic Andes Mountains that stand behind the church as a backdrop.

Our time in the hotel lasted only a few months. One Sunday morning I watched a Jesuit priest come and stand in the entrance to our room during our service. His eyes roved around as if he was taking pictures. The next day, Monday, I was called by the hotel to inform me that regretfully they could no longer accommodate us.

"Is it a matter of money?" I inquired.

"Very sorry," was the only response I received.

Thus began a period of time of meeting in other hotels and diverse places—not to mention our return to Canada for a year of furlough. We left the church in the hands of a missionary colleague and Sergio.

Furlough in Canada 1985–1986

Air Nicaragua

On the way back to Canada with the kids in August of 1985, we had decided to stop off in Costa Rica to visit some of the friends we had made during our year of language study. There are no direct flights from Chile to Costa Rica, and the best connection we could make was changing planes in Panama. We opted, as we often do, for the cheapest airline from Panama to San José, Costa Rica, which was Air Nicaragua.

Our adventure began as we changed planes in the Panama airport. We did not have much time to make the transfer, and I made the wrong choice of directions and took the family far away from our boarding lounge. Keep in mind we have all our baggage for a year's stay in Canada with us. When we discovered my error, we panicked and began to retrace our steps all the while hearing that dreadful announcement, "This is the last call for Air Nicaragua: all passengers should be on the plane."

I don't remember how we made it, but I have a vivid image in my mind of how we must have looked running disheveled up to the departure gate.

I was surprised to see how few passengers there were on this flight. All of us were relieved to have the plane door closed with us on the inside; we began our take-off. While the plane was still gaining altitude, a man stood up at the front of the plane and began to make what we thought was to be an announcement. Up to this moment I had heard no mention of San José or Costa Rica only that this plane was en route to Managua, capital of Nicaragua. It is to be remembered that, in 1985, the revolution was very much alive, and Nicaragua was controlled by a Communist dictatorship.

I began to shudder, thinking that perhaps, in our panic, we had boarded the wrong plane. This would have been no small error and could have had dire consequences. Our passports were last stamped in Chile, a military dictatorship involved in a civil war with the communists. The man began a political speech extolling all the virtues of the people's popular revolution of Nicaragua. Because we lived under a dictatorship at the time, we knew something about control and police. Visions of landing without proper documentation and of being detained as political prisoners burst forth in my mind.

This speech more or less took our attention away from the flight, and as suddenly as he had begun, he finished and sat down. We landed in San José with no further notice. Everyone got off the plane which continued on empty except for the orator, to Managua. We were eager for some relaxation and enjoyed our time in Costa Rica. All too soon we left to journey to Regina, Saskatchewan, which would be our home for the next twelve months.

Tour Stories

I only toured in Ontario once. It was the fall of 1985 and a very special time visiting some very special and supportive churches. One home where I stayed was that of a wealthy business man. He lent me his Mazda RX7, and not just for the days I was in his church; he told me to keep it for the entire tour and gave me his credit card to buy gas! Thankfully, I managed not to get a speeding ticket!

After Ontario I toured in the Maritimes. I had heard about the fall colours in the deciduous forest and had seen pictures, but I arrived just in time to see with my own eyes a beauty I will never forget. I remember coming in for the landing in Halifax. It was like descending into a bed of multicoloured umbrellas that slowly turned into trees.

The warmth and hospitality of these folks was second to none, but what stands out in my mind is a record I set there that never to be surpassed. One day I spoke eleven times. The details are no longer vivid except for the moment I returned to my billet. I had only the strength to crawl into bed; not even the energy to undress. I *think* I took my shoes off!

One of my tours took me to the bustling metropolis of Shaunavon, in southwest Saskatchewan. This was in 1986, and the tour date was around Valentine's Day. The day before I was to leave to drive there, the weather turned cold, bitterly cold. I believe we hit lows of 50 below and that was the daytime temperature—when I left the temperature was below minus 40. Needless to say, the heater was not sufficient to heat the car, and it was cold. In fact, it was so cold that I used an ice scraper on the *inside* of the windows to keep the ice build-up off. I remember being concerned about my safety but not concerned enough to call them and cancel the meeting.

Colin Driving

My son Colin will forgive his dad for saying that he is not a natural with machines. He is so very good at many other things—but driving, not so much. A few months before we were to return for our second term in Chile we realized that we should perhaps look into getting Colin's driver's license. He would soon be sixteen. We applied and got his learner's license, and I began to give him lessons. One day we were driving out on the highway north of Regina where the flat prairie dips down into a valley. Colin was at the wheel of our standard shift Ford and down we went with no problem. Beginning to go up on the other side the car began to slow down and nearly stalled. Colin, in some distress said, "Dad there is something wrong with the car, it is stopping." This was a prairie boy's first encounter driving on anything other than flat land. Of course, going up, you needed to shift down. Lesson learned.

BJ Stays in Canada

Our year in Canada seemed to fly by. The boys settled into school, and we settled into our respective routines, doing our best to make Regina our home again. The elephant in the room was the decision we would have to make regarding Brandon. It was the fall of 1986, and he was just entering grade twelve, and it did not seem the right thing to do to take him back to Quito for one year and then back to Canada to attend university.

It seems easy enough to say it now, but the wrenching in my gut as I write reminds me it was anything but easy. We always seemed to have a plan to make the difficult decisions easier. They never did! This time Brandon was to accompany his adopted family to a summer camp, and we would go and spend the first night there with them all. It should have been exciting; they had horses, all kinds of activities. I managed not to cry but hated every moment as I could not forget what we were about to do.

Unfortunately, things with Brandon did not get better after we returned to Chile. Brandon had a hard time and didn't stay with the family long after we had left him, choosing instead to go on his own. He didn't do well. We carried around a great deal of guilt and self-recrimination over Brandon's struggles, which only added to our sorrow and pain.

Santiago 1986–1990

Las Acacias

Change is inevitable. When we returned to Chile, we sensed that things had changed but were not overly alarmed. Of course, it had changed, we had been absent for a year. Nevertheless looking back now we should have recognized some signs of the coming storms. We soon found it necessary to leave this new facility and again faced the urgent and basic need to find a new location. This time we were led, out of necessity, to the Jalils' garage. Before jumping to pictures of the typical North American garage packed full of stuff and with its double lifting doors, let me remind you that the Jalils lived, at that time, in the former Polish Embassy. The garage was large enough to hold two of the largest Mercedes Benz limousines. They were removed on Sundays to enable us to set up chairs and a pulpit. In fact, I remember using the grape arbor that grew along the lattice work on one side of the garage as an object lesson while we served communion. It was altogether lovely as a temporary location. We knew however that we would have to find another location before the cold of winter. God, who is always on time, provided us with a new hotel.

Las Acacias, a quaint hotel would turn out to be the last non-permanent home for the Cordillera church. We had moved three times prior to moving into Las Acacias, which our mentor Walter later said was, in itself, something of a miracle. "That a church can exist and grow for six years without a permanent home is unheard of."

Shortly after beginning in our new locality, God began to pour out His Spirit on us, resulting in many baptisms. All this would not go without opposition, and the most painful kind is that which comes from within.

Opposition from Within

The feeling that things had changed during our year in Canada was soon confirmed by way of warnings from several of the members of the church. "Watch out for Sergio," they warned me. Sergio was my friend and colleague, and I defended him.

I remember the day I first made contact with Carlos of El Trio Mar del Plata. This Argentinian musical group had achieved considerable fame and popularity throughout Latin America, Canada and the USA.

In spite of many ups and downs we remained absolutely resolute in our determination to do everything within our means to advance our vision of a large noticeable church for the upper middle class.

An unfortunate chapter in the life of the church—and for me, a particularly painful one—was the betrayal, in October of 1986, by our good friends Sergio and Ingrid. We had been warned after returning from our furlough year in Canada that things had changed. We refused to believe that our friends would do anything either to harm us or more importantly damage the church which is the body of Christ. We were wrong on both counts.

The issues were more complicated than I care to deal with, but the one thing that could not be avoided had to do with my determination to be an evangelistic church. We had just been given a promising gift from God in the form of this magnificent world renowned group, El Trio Mar del Plata whose main focus was in presenting the gospel through their music. Sergio and Ingrid believed this music was satanic.

(In the traditional missions model the Chileans would have been in charge and our vision would have died with this rebellion.)

I could have compromised many things; evangelism I was not prepared to forgo. I remember the words of Sergio. "Doug no one is going to come to an evangelistic campaign, and no one will respond to a call and we will all look silly."

I have been foolish so many times in my life that it really meant nothing to me if the campaign failed—at least we would have been obedient to our mandate to go into all the world and preach the gospel. I remained adamant, which I am sure led to one of the worst periods of my life.

The following Sunday, a few weeks before the Trio were to come for their campaign, it was Sergio's turn to preach in the church. Several people loyal to us came and said, "Please Doug don't let him preach; he is going to betray you."

He had chosen for his text that morning Revelation 2:12–16. My heart sank. Sergio is quite tall for a Chilean, taller than I am. In the pulpit he is formidable. As he began, I changed seats and sat beside Horacio, a young university student who I was very close to. "Horacio," I said, "please take notes. I believe we will need them."

> "And to the angel of the church in Pergamum write:
>
> The One who has the sharp two-edged sword says this: I know where you dwell, where Satan's throne is; and you hold fast My name, and did not deny My faith even in the days of Antipas, My witness, My faithful one, who was killed among you, where Satan dwells.

But I have a few things against you, because you have there some who hold the teaching of Balaam, who kept teaching Balak to put a stumbling block before the sons of Israel, to eat things sacrificed to idols and to commit *acts of* immorality.

So you also have some who in the same way hold the teaching of the Nicolaitans. Therefore repent; or else I am coming to you quickly, and I will make war against them with the sword of My mouth.

[Rev 2:12–16]

Certain phrases from this passage will help you to understand what he said that morning. Let me explain:

I was being equated with the Nicolaitians. He made it clear that this church was apostate and permitted wicked things to happen. Then he made reference to Satan living in our midst and said, "We all know who that is," as he pointed towards me.

In shock, I don't remember much else, except that he finished by violently slamming his Bible shut and storming down the centre aisle out of the church.

This was communion Sunday. I was devastated. How do you go on after that let alone lead the congregation in one of the most sacred acts of faith? Only God knows how I did it. Only God could have enabled me to have grace and love not only towards the congregation who had all been brutalized, but also for Sergio. I have seen him as a victim of his own legalism.

If only that had been the end of it. After the service, we found Sergio campaigning in the parking lot. We were subsequently cited to attend a congregational meeting that Wednesday.

My heart was aching, yet in spite of the fear and pain, I knew the church, the vision and the future of Cordillera were at stake and would need to be defended.

God led so clearly and so easily in the next few days. I felt that in addition to everything else this was actually a power struggle. The next few days would confirm my suspicions. Sergio and his father wanted nothing less than to take over the church, which had recently begun to grow in numbers and reputation. The Sunday of the insurrection we were approximately one hundred people.

The issue to be forced was, "Can missionaries pastor a National Church?" The then-president of the National Church was not at all in favour and, true to form, the mission did not support us, but by God's provision he was away on several weeks' vacation, and the vice president was a personal friend, and when I asked his opinion he said, "You need to obtain a letter from the National Church supporting you as pastor of Cordillera."

"How do I do that?" I asked.

"Do you have a pen?" He began to dictate a letter which I would then send to him and to which he would reply.

All this transpired miraculously in a three-day period—as the office of the National church was located in Temuco nearly five hundred miles south. Again I do not remember how, but I had this reply in my suit pocket when we attended the congregational meeting Wednesday evening.

Two opposing armies could not have developed more animosity than we felt in that room. The one hundred had divided into roughly eighty versus twenty, and we were the underdogs. Back and forth it went: charges mainly against my character and my actions. I remember at one point Ofelia, who is a lady of the highest class and position, shouted out at Ingrid, *Cerdo!* [Pig!]. Never before—or after—did I witness anything close to her outburst that day as she watched and listened while people slandered her pastor. This was probably the closest things came to violence, and it was at this point that Sergio and his supporters played their trump card.

"*You* are no longer pastor of the church. I am Chilean and am taking over from you as you cannot legally be the pastor."

Now the rat was out. I recognized it for what it was, and it had little to do with the type of music. Sergio had grown accustomed during our year on furlough to being in charge, and he was not going to let me resume authority, pure and simple.

Inside I was rejoicing with the joy and confidence that can only come from knowing that God is on your side.

"No," I replied, "I *am* the pastor of Cordillera, and I am not going anywhere. You clearly have choices. You are welcome to stay with us with me as the pastor of the church, or you can leave together with those who support you and begin your own church—but I am pastor of the Cordillera."

From several of them came shouts of: "You can't stay. It is illegal. We are now the leaders of Cordillera."

I chose then to pull the envelope from my breast pocket and begin to read. Silence fell on the one side of the room while cries of "Halleluiah!" erupted from the other. I don't remember if I had finished reading before they left. Next Sunday we were fewer than twenty members, but I was still the pastor.

A New Strategy

At this time we did not appreciate or even consider that what we were doing and how we were doing it was breaking new ground in mission strategy. We had no strategy except to rely totally on God's daily leading.

The fact the church and our goals were not destroyed in the takeover was due to one profound difference in our procedure—I was the pastor of the church! While it seems inconsequential it was fundamental in ensuring the church continued towards its goal of being visible, large and directed towards the upper middle class in Chile, people who were largely ignored by the mission and were without access to the basic gospel truths.

Contextualization of our message was a default result of getting close to all our Chilean friends. This was certainly done at the expense of not having as close relationships with our missionary colleagues, many of whom, we felt, were trying to preserve their own cultural comfort. This was illustrated in what was eaten, celebrating national holidays and spending much time with each other.

In contrast we did not see the great need to produce peanut butter nor to insist on importing turkeys for special holidays, and we often missed out on birthday celebrations of our colleagues in order to participate in the lives of our national friends.

We had learned of the importance of prayer—again not due to particularly pious behaviour but rather by default as described in our weekly visits to Santiago while we were still assigned to Viña del Mar.

In addition I had not been raised in any church environment and had no predetermined idea of expectant or liturgical behaviour. I was prone to taking at face value what I read in scripture and applying it as best I could. In fact, I was offended whenever we were invited to a prayer meeting and the prayer was the least important aspect of the gathering.

We developed better relations with Chilean pastors than our missionary colleagues although that is a generalization. We found them more open to actually praying with us when we met 'for prayer.'

We did have a fairly well-defined goal of how to "do church." Perhaps from my banking background, I was a pragmatist. The task at hand was to teach as many as much about Jesus as we could. It was patently obvious this could only be done through multiplication which fit exactly into our understanding of the Great Commission which is to go and make disciples.

We began to spend time with a responsive few with the goal of preparing these disciples to be disciple makers as well. The fact that we targeted our discipleship at the upper class was not only innovative but both scorned and resisted at the time by both the mission and much of the National Church.

Piro and Her Family

One of the first families to commit themselves to the new Cordillera Church was the family of Oscar and Chichi Poseck and their three children, Piro, Scarlette and Oscar Angelo. They would invite us often to have supper with them, and I am convinced there is no better cook in all of Chile than Chichi!

Perhaps the fact we had two handsome sons about the same age as their two girls had something to do with this at the beginning, as we were included just as if we were part of their family. We even spent one summer holiday, the four of us with the five of them at their summer cottage in the south of Chile at a lake called Lican Ray.

The south of Chile is renowned for its beauty, and this lake is particularly blessed with its clean white sand and view of Villarrica Volcano in the distance. We also spent one New Years with them at this same house and had a real eye opener as to how they celebrate. Food is central to most Chilean celebrations, and I remember they hired someone to come early in the afternoon of New Year's Eve to start a huge outdoor barbeque. In due time once the coals were ready a half a lamb appeared skewered on a steel rod some three to four meters long. The next six hours it was gently turned and basted with a mixture of olive oil, white wine and garlic.

Just as we thought we had the menu figured out, and were licking our lips anticipating some lamb ribs, the ladies began to assemble tables and by ten or so other food began to parade out of the kitchen. Salads by the score including some Chilean specialties; a salad called *ensalada chilena* which is made with sliced onion and tomato marinated in lemon and olive oil blended together. Another made with avocado and celery in the same kind of marinade. Then a huge selection of cold cooked vegetables. Delicious!

Soon some fresh bread arrived and farmer sausage went on the barbeque grill. We were encouraged to help ourselves and our arms were twisted to ensure we did so. Always keeping in mind there would be lamb at some point, we did hold back a little room, but our best intentions were blown away when huge steaks were added to the grill: T-bone steaks, cooked to perfection, at least one for each person present.

We were not huge wine drinkers, but we were introduced to a seasonal drink that evening. Fresh strawberries had been soaked in red wine for a couple of days. As we enjoyed this exquisite beverage, we wondered how many missionaries had even heard of such a thing.

I am not sure how we managed to eat as much as we did. Thinking back I still can imagine the contradiction of being tempted to eat more, enjoying it, and then feeling so uncomfortably full. I do know that when we finally poured ourselves into bed at four in the morning, we all went immediately to sleep. No one moved until ten the next morning.

We arose to coffee, bacon and eggs, fresh rolls—and that was just to get us ready to finish off what had been left over from the night before!

One of my lasting delights is the relationships Ann and I made with Piro. She came from a difficult home situation, and we fell in love with each other. She would come and spend hours with Ann and me, hungry to learn more of God. Her family also grew to be one of our closest allies and friends. I miss them dreadfully. Piro is like a daughter to me.

She loved us enough to help us improve our Spanish. She taught us a tremendous amount about Chilean culture. Then Brandon came to live in Chile for a time, and she became even more important to us.

Café con Piernas

One could speculate that over eighty percent of business in Chile was conducted in small coffee shops known as cafés con piernas—literally coffee with legs which is a good description. There were dozens if not hundreds of these little hole-in-the-wall shops each one with its own decor but all with the same distinction. Serving the many varieties of espresso, lattés and Americanos were young attractive girls with skirts as short as decency would allow—sometimes even shorter!

I am sure we were judged by some for frequenting these establishments, but our Chilean friends found it normal and comfortable to talk business here rather than in the typical office or home context we were used to.

Baptisms

The church continued to grow, and with growth came the need to serve more people in diverse ways. We had our first baptism. Never have I performed a "normal" baptism. An entire chapter could be written just on baptisms. The first to be baptized in the Cordillera was Maria Mercedes. Her story has been written and published in the Alliance Witness under the title of "A Bird in a Gilded Cage."

Maria Mercedes was there at the first Bible study in Ophelia's home. As I have done so many times in my life with others, I misjudged her and actually complained to God about her. Maria had been the wife of a former Chilean ambassador to the United States. Now divorced, she lived alone. When we met her, she was under the care and guidance of five psychologists. She was taking so many drugs to keep her going that some of the time she didn't know if she was in Chile or the States. She was incapable of eating or drinking on her own and was accustomed to wearing a food bib.

Unkindly I thought at first, *Why me Lord? We are trying to start a church here. Is this really foundational discipleship material? I don't think so.* Well I was wrong. Categorically wrong.

I don't remember formally praying for Maria or laying hands on her, yet week by week, as she read the word of God, she began to improve. The first time I watched her on her own take a cup of hot coffee to her mouth, I stared, imagining that she would spill or burn herself—but she did not.

Then her speech began to improve. I am a strong believer in memorization of the Word of God. I didn't really expect Maria to be able to do that, but not only was she able, she excelled.

The morning of her baptism she demonstrated her prowess with the Sword of the Spirit—the Bible. We were offered the use of another church's baptismal tank and joined them that morning. The time for her baptism came, and I helped Maria into the tank in her white, floor length baptismal gown.

After asking her the usual questions regarding her salvation, I invited her to say a few words. There we were standing nearly waist deep in water. Maria grabbed the microphone from me before I knew it and began to quote verses. How many? I don't know because she spoke so fast. I think the only way you could determine how many verses she quoted would be to time it to see how many verses could be quoted without drawing a breath!

As quickly as she began, she ended, throwing the mike in my general direction as she threw herself backwards. Oh no! If I drop this mike into the water we may all be electrocuted. If I don't reach down to Maria who is quickly sinking to the bottom and soon will be laying on her back in three feet of water she will drown. The choice was horrible: death by electrocution or drowning?

Fortunately, she held her breath long enough for me to safely dispose of the microphone and reach down and drag her to the surface. The smile on Maria's face as she came up to the surface epitomizes what I perceive in Romans 6:5 *For if we have become united with Him in the likeness of His death, certainly we shall also be in the likeness of His resurrection.* The look on Maria's face as she emerged from following her Lord in Baptism was nothing less than angelic.

Maria holds the honour of being the first member to be baptized in the Cordillera Church. I think she still holds the honorary position of being the best example of God's grace and mercy as well. Maria, like Abraham, never did see the promised land of a Cordillera church building. She never doubted it would happen. A few years later I celebrated her funeral, naming her, "the first lady of Cordillera." She had been a follower of Christ for only a short number of years, yet her life was exemplary. Who among us can count seven generations of believers as a result of our lives?

The church was packed for the funeral. People from all walks of life were there, many from the media who came not as professionals but as friends. Tears flowed freely that afternoon—mine among them—as we imagined the reunion already taking place in heaven between Maria Mercedes now fully whole, never again to suffer pain, seeing clearly for the first time her Saviour Jesus Christ. I looked over the congregation and counted no less than thirteen souls, now themselves followers of Jesus Christ because of the witness and example of Maria. *Thank you Lord*, I thought, *for a life well lived. Forgive me Lord for being so blind to your ways.*

We baptized on such a regular basis that it almost became part of our liturgy. Finish preaching by ten thirty so that we can meet at the hotel pool and start the baptisms. Finish, if possible, by eleven in order to hold a reception for the new believers in our new hotel Las Acacias.

With every baptism, death, and funeral, our sorrow at not having a place of our own grew. Only God knew our pain, and only God could provide the solution.

One baptism that must be recalled was that of Blanquita, a slight woman with an impressive presence for her eighty-six years. We met Blanquita at one of our new Bible Studies. When she came to know Jesus as her Saviour, she told us her life story.

She came from a very wealthy and influential family. At her very first Bible Study, she taught us something about aristocracy. She didn't wait to be introduced to the others; she did it herself.

"Who are you, dearie?" she began as she went around the table one by one asking the same question. As soon as the others had revealed their two last names which every Chilean has, she told them hers. It was like playing a trump card in bridge. "I am Blanquita, etc. etc. etc." Her two last names rang out like names from a history book of the who's who in Chile. There was nothing pretentious about it. She was simply stating facts, and those facts told all the others, "I am now top dog here."

In the weeks to follow she went on to tell us all of her story, how as a little girl of six she and her sister would spend summers at the family farm. There amidst the family lands, vineyards and animals she could enjoy her freedom and innocence as a child.

One Sunday morning, she recalled, she and her sister went down to where the family that provided labour for the farm lived. They were drawn by the sound of voices and music. They went closer and closer and finally worked up the courage to pull themselves up and look over the windowsill. The family that lived there were evangelicals and that very word "evangelical" had coined a new phrase in Chile: Canuto, a derogatory word that was associated with the poor.

Entranced by something they heard or felt, they were compelled to return each Sunday to listen. Then during the rest of the week, Blanquita and her sister would pull the covers over themselves at night supposing no one could hear and sing the songs they heard. It was not long before their mother caught them and asked, "Where did you learn those songs?" Upon their confession they were ordered never to return to that house.

Now, eighty years later, God in His faithfulness was rewarding the faith of a little girl and explaining to her what it was that those people had and that she wanted and needed, which was a personal relationship with Jesus. The next step was baptism.

At eighty-six Blanquita was very frail. I am sure she didn't weigh more than eighty pounds. She was to be the first baptism in our new hotel location. I had arranged with the owners to let half the water out of the only pool open during the winter season. It was a very deep pool perhaps six feet at the shallow end.

Early on the morning of the baptism I went early to the hotel and out to see the pool. To my dismay they had forgotten to let any water out. What to do? In the time we had, there was no way we could let sufficient water out to make much of a difference, so I came up with a solution. We would sink a table into the pool and stand on the table. Yes I know, not very bright.

We made big deals of baptisms, using them to introduce friends and family to this new faith called Protestantism. Blanquita came down the path, dressed in her white robe which bunched up around her legs. It was the smallest robe we had and still probably four sizes too big for diminutive Blanquita . At this time my only concern was that the cold wouldn't kill her.

Shortly after she arrived, I stepped into the pool and found my balance on the table. I found out later that wiser colleagues of mine saw the danger at this point and began divesting themselves of watches and wallets in order to be able to dive in and help us. Blanquita was helped to get down the ladder to join me on the table. Just as soon as they could no longer help her from pool side I reached out from my precarious perch on the table.

At best, a long robe catches some air, but one that is much too large is like a huge balloon. As Blanquita stepped down by faith to join me on my table submerged in six feet of water, her feet went out from under her and up she floated to the gasps of all around. Do you know what happens when the air is suddenly let out of a balloon? Feet up in the air, simultaneous loss of buoy-ancy and down she went. The table rocked. We somehow caught our balance and the baptism went on without further incident. Blanquita nearly set a Guinness world record for the shortest time between a baptism and a funeral.

We had many other baptisms. Once, it was rainy and very cold, and I was called at home by the baptismal candidates early in the morning before I left for the church. The question of course was, "Pastor are we going to go through with this today in spite of the cold?"

I don't know it was faith or stupidity that caused me to answer, "Yes, of course."

That day it poured and with the wind howling down from the snow-laden Cordillera Mountains it was very cold. We prayed that God would glorify Himself, and at the precise moment when we walked out of the church down the path to the pool the sun came out! So as to ensure absolutely that we knew this to be a gift and sign from our Heavenly Father, *the sun shone only on the area of the pool and only during the time of the baptism.* As we walked back to the church, the rain closed in behind us, and the wind and rain prevailed the rest of the day.

Then there was a summer baptism with no shortage of heat and sun. The problem that day was an infestation of a bother-some flying insect very common to Chile. Although they are not poisonous, they swarm and get in your mouth and ears. The lady candidates, while putting on a brave face, did not want to go outside. I remember again the specific prayer. *Father God as you did in Egypt would you remove these insects that are bothering your people and interfering with this testimony of faith.* Sure enough, a breeze sprang up, and the insects disappeared. It was a glorious testimony. No wonder that the baptisms at Cordillera were also considered evangelistic times. Anyone present could not deny the presence of God. Each one was supernatural.

El Trio Mar del Plata

It is a funny thing perhaps, but I count the real birth of the Cordillera church to be that Wednesday of the church split. After the division, the church began to grow rapidly adding new believers every week. The growth was not without painful moments and times of testing such as the first evangelistic campaign with El Trio Mar del Plata scheduled for some three weeks after the church split; but the rapid growth continued.

The Trio, although Argentinian, did not arrive from Argentina, but from Brussels on their way home from participating in a Billy Graham conference on evangelism. The week before they had a congregation of over 10,000 people. Our entire congregation of twenty was less than half of one percent of that number.

My worst expectations were confirmed the first night of the campaign, and it was a moment of deep testing. Whom were we serving? Who were we trying to please? Not one person other than the few missionaries and their families came that night. I was desolate. My respect and gratitude for this group took a giant step forward that evening, when the leader, Carlos, came up to me after they had packed up their equipment. He came and stood beside me put his arm around me and said, "Dougie don't worry."

I had tears in my eyes. "But Carlos I feel guilty that we are taking up your valuable time. You could be somewhere else ministering to thousands."

Carlos' consoling reply began yet another learning curve in my life. "Dougie, we didn't come here because you asked us. We came here because God commanded us, and further we will keep coming back as often as you invite and as often as we can."

True to their word they have become an integral part in the growth of the Cordillera church and, as you will read later, they very fittingly were part of the worldwide Alliance meetings that took place in Santiago 2008 in the Hotel Sheraton!

The Three Crucifixions

When the dust of the church split had settled, it was clear that the division had been largely down family lines. Sergio and Ingrid had taken with them all who were related to them and their friends—except the Poseck family to whom I am forever indebted. I know they paid a price for staying with us in a country where family ties are so important.

About a week after the congregational meeting, I was summoned to the mission office to talk to the field chairman about what had happened. In my naïveté I thought he was going to commiserate with me, perhaps pray for my broken heart. I had no idea that I was to be held responsible and indeed blamed for this division. I had been devastated when the warnings about Sergio had become reality. He had been my friend, perhaps my best friend up to that time. I missed those who had left. Now I was being blamed.

Not long after this I was called before the whole of the field leadership. They grilled me about what had happened and made it quite clear that this had been a blow to the entire National Church and that I was responsible. There was talk of lost tithes, loss of members, and particularly this one family that had such a long history in the church.

I don't know how much I said. Probably not much as I was still in shock and trying to get on with the task at hand. I do know that this was a time when God truly poured out His mercy on the church. God entrusted to us so many new converts. There was so much to do, and here we were wasting time on what, to me, was spilt milk.

I am sure it was my lack of repentance that led to the final crucifixion. The mission never did agree with our goal to reach the upper class nor our methods for doing so. However at this meeting the mission did not count on Ann. She had watched what was happening without saying anything. The leaders mistakenly took her silence as agreeing with them. One should not assume.

We met that morning and went through the same perfunctory things, like praying for God's leading and blessing. Then quickly they jumped to their agenda.

"You are responsible for a great deal of harm to individuals and to the National Church and to the Mission."

I could hear noise like buzzing in my ear but could not make out words until Ann cut them off. "You are right you would not have this problem if Doug had not been here. Neither would you have this great church that is growing faster than any other church in Chile. You should be congratulating Doug and supporting him instead of this disgraceful way you have been treating him and us. I see his tears. I see his pain. You should be *ashamed* of yourselves."

I have never been more proud of anyone in my life. I heard every word *she* said! I don't think it should come as a surprise to you that later, when we had returned to Canada, we received a letter from the mission telling us we would not be welcomed back to Chile. I am sure they had already made that decision that day but lacked the valour to tell us to our faces. As a result of their callousness, we lost all our household things that we had been gathering for nearly ten years. Such is the price for no compromise.

Rapid Growth

God's ways are surely not our ways. In the physical sense these were some of the hardest days of my life. I see clearly now that God kept me afloat for His glory. I don't think I have ever spent a period of my life spiritually closer to my Lord than during the last months of our time in Chile.

The church launched into evangelism. We had the blessed cooperation of the Trio. Then we began to do Evangelism Explosion. In a congregation of fewer than twenty we managed to have up to three teams of evangelists.

Coincidently God brought to Chile, that summer, a world renowned evangelist. At first we thought he was misinformed or did not realize Chile was in the southern hemisphere when we heard he was coming in January. The Chileans refer to January and February as the long weekend of the year. Such is that state in the capital that about forty percent of the population leaves on vacation and the streets are nearly empty.

What was going to happen to this evangelistic crusade? Would even one person show up? To further complicate things they had rented nothing less than the National Stadium which holds nearly 50,000 people! Well what can you do? We decided to help out as best we could.

The first day of the campaign arrived, and we went down early to help with ushering and counselling. We all received a lesson on the sovereign will of God that evening. First the stadium filled up! Where had all these people come from? Then the message began, a simple gospel message. Through the translation we wondered how effective it would be. Next, well before the end of the message and before the call to salvation was made, people began to rise up out of their seats spontaneously and move towards the altar in the centre of the field.

In the three days of that campaign over 20,000 people made first time decisions for Jesus!

Certainly a good number of churches had been involved in the planning, but clearly this had been an act of God. A follow-up meeting had been scheduled for two days after the campaign. At this meeting, the results were first announced, and we would have all rejoiced except there were only a small handful of churches represented. How were we going to follow-up this multitude?

Each name had been recorded on a computer printout. The old kind on continuous feed perforated paper. The stack of paper was intimidating. Our turn came. How many sheets can you take? By faith I said three. Each page held thirty contacts. If our church could contact half that number and draw them in, our church family would triple!

So we began. We were all eager but at the same time none of us had fully gotten over the tremendous pain that the split had caused. The story of the first night of Evangelism Explosion visits bears telling.

We gathered at our house in Vitacura around seven thirty to pray. There were five of us, so we divided into two teams and each group took three names and addresses and off we went. Ninety names given at random. Six names picked off those sheets. Five souls going off into the dark of a city of five million souls.

Ann and I had no contact at our first address. We hurried on to the second, mildly discouraged. The second home invited us in warmly. In a few minutes we heard the story of a grown man who, as a youth, had wandered away from his roots as the son of a pastor in one of our churches. I knew his father! We shared many stories together making sure that he had assurance of his salvation. I was watching the time and knew we had to leave shortly in order to get home in time to receive the other team for our debriefing.

As we stood to leave the man asked us if we could do him a favour. We said if it were possible we would be glad. He told us a heartbreaking story of his daughter, Patty, who had just had a baby and her husband had walked out on her. Would we visit her? Gulp, we would never get through our ninety contacts at this rate.

"Of course," we said.

We arrived home only minutes before the other team. Our excitement was met by theirs as they began to share with us of their visits. Their first address had no answer, but the second family let them in. They had not had a good experience there as it seemed the family wanted to teach them and tell them all about their own faith and experience. Somehow gracefully they excused themselves and moved on to their last address where they had a divine encounter.

They told us how this sweet young lady had prayed with tears to receive Christ as her Saviour. With tears themselves they spoke of the faithfulness of God to lead them to this woman in her hour of need. The hairs on my neck began to rise as they told the story of a young woman whose husband had just abandoned her with a new baby.

"Is her name Patty?" I asked.

"How did you know?" They were in awe. What are the odds that one of our two teams would visit the house of the daughter of the family we had just promised to visit? Of course, we know that a God of love will do the miraculous to insure those who want to find Him are indeed found.

God so encouraged us that evening that we went out many more times with joy and thanksgiving in our hearts.

Trip to New Zealand 1987

My mother remarried in 1975 to one of my father's good friends—a man he had met in a POW camp in Germany. As the man was a Kiwi, they decided to move to Auckland. While most of this decision was positive, part of the downside was the distance. I had not seen her since the wedding—over twelve years earlier.

Mom sent me money to purchase a plane ticket, and I made arrangements to go. This was going to be a very long trip even though I would be leaving from the same southern hemisphere. During the '80s many countries had embargoes on Chile, and no Chilean airline could fly into New Zealand at that time.

Thus began another adventure. First stop, Easter Island. There was a two hour layover and an opportunity to have a tour of this small island; the touring to be done from the back of old jeeps at a cost of sixty dollars per person. Most of the passengers said no thanks. Then to convince ourselves that we had made the right decision we made fun of the dust plumes that the jeeps made as they did a tour that did not reach more than a kilometre from the airport.

Next stop was Tahiti. What a gorgeous island. Gem of the Pacific. A jewel set in an emerald sea. This trip was a tremendous gift that I could never have afforded on my own. The prices were outlandish. The hotel we stayed at had its own dock from which we could see the large number of French warships stationed nearby. I remember the clarity of the water: it was like looking at the bottom of the ocean without any water it was so clear. I had twelve hours in paradise before boarding New Zealand Air for the last leg of the trip.

I had two wonderful weeks in Auckland with Mom and John, her husband. They took me to see all the sights and the time went very quickly.

I was looking forward to the trip home and again stopping over in Tahiti. I remember that I was scheduled to fly out on my least favourite airplane: an L-1011. I say this because of the characteristic flapping of the wings. They are engineered with so much flexibility that, on takeoff, it appears that the plane has a will of its own to assist in the take off by moving the wings up and down. We were all aboard on time and waiting to leave, but there was some hold up and we sat in our seats without moving for forty-five minutes. The pilot apologized several times and finally announced we were clear to go and we taxied out to the apron. There we stopped again. When we hadn't moved for another fifteen minutes or so we knew something was wrong, and again the pilot came on and advised us we were returning to the ramp due to a warning light showing a possible wheel problem.

We sat and waited again with nervous noise growing in the aircraft. I can hardly believe this now as I write, but to help pass the time they piped in the local news on our TV screen. It was a documentary describing a recurring problem with the engines on—you guessed it—the L-1011. This in addition to already being anxious and sitting in our seats without being able to move for going on two hours.

Up to now I wasn't worried about missing my connecting flight to Chile, but I was not appreciating losing hours in my new found paradise. When it was announced that we were going to be transferred to another aircraft, there were shouts of relief and we couldn't get off that plane fast enough.

Thus we arrived some two and a half hours late in Tahiti. The scheduled transportation to take us from the airport to the hotel was long gone. Not to worry. I saw myself as a seasoned traveler, and, although I spoke no French, I found a small bus and made inquiries using the name of our hotel. The driver, a woman, spoke some English and assured me the bus was going to that hotel.

The short version is she lied. I knew nothing about this island and it was a total surprise when we turned into the Hyatt Regent Hotel—not my hotel at all. It was much more than a surprise when the driver held her hand out looking for money before I got off the bus. My transport was already paid for and beside I had no francs.

Finally she gave up on me as a bad job and I entered the hotel. I began to explain my dilemma to a less than helpful staff. Was this really a four star hotel? I asked if I could use their phone and was shocked when they didn't even answer but pointed to a payphone in the lobby. Again I reminded them I had no francs and they had not been willing to exchange a few dollars for me. Cold silence. They wouldn't even look at me.

Now I was truly angry. I took up my suit bag and began dragging my suitcase behind me up to the closest road. I would hitchhike, I thought. I didn't even know which direction! I was delivered by a shining knight mounted in a white step-van. He was a painter. He knew no English and I no French, but I repeated the name of the hotel enough times until he began to answer very enthusiastically "Oui oui oui." He did in fact drive me straight to my hotel where I was received like a long lost brother. All the other "less experienced travellers" had arrived some time earlier.

Missed Flight

I returned to Canada in June of 1987 to attend Brandon's graduation. It was a difficult time as I sensed that he was not in a very good frame of mind. Although a necessary visit, it was not an enjoyable time.

Perhaps an incident on my way to Regina was foreboding of the difficulty I would experience there. Before getting to Regina, after a couple of days stop-over in Toronto, our friends drove me to the airport at what I believed to be four hours before the flight. I didn't even hurry to check in, rather I sauntered.

At the check-in counter I had one of "those" experiences. The attendant looked at my ticket and then back at me. She again looked at the ticket and then said, "Sir, your plane has already left."

I explained, mainly from fear and shock, "That can't be. I am early."

"Oh no," she replied, "If you look out there," pointing out the window to a plane just taking off, "that is your plane."

I had somehow mixed up the arrival time in Vancouver with the departure time in Toronto, and due to three time zones, I missed the plane. I guess the right amount of dejection has merits because as I stood there crestfallen and bewildered, she hailed a supervisor who came over and took pity on me. As a favour, they got me on a subsequent flight.

After returning from Brandon's grad, we continued to hear that he was really struggling, and lost all contact with him for nearly a whole year.

During that time we prayed and hoped and waited to hear from him. Ann and I expected that one day we would get a telephone call either from the police or a hospital, giving us the bad news that something had happened to him

In fact the call came one night in June of 1988 around two in the morning. Ann took the call and heard that it was Brandon and threw the phone to me. She missed one of the most beautiful calls a parent could ever have. Brandon wanted us to know that he had rededicated his life to Jesus. Then, as if that news was not sufficiently wonderful he said, "Dad I have made a mess of things. Would it be all right if I come to Chile for a year and have you disciple me?"

Peter Paratrooper

Through some distant family connection in the church, we were invited to visit Peter. We knew that he was one of the elite personal guards of President Pinochet. In fact, he told us that he helped train them.

We had a little difficulty finding the house in the dark of night—but eventually did—and we marched up to the front door and rang the bell. No one answered so we knocked and rang again. Finally a maid came to the door to inform us that unfortunately "Don" Peter was sick and couldn't see anyone.

A little disappointed—but not dismayed as this happens frequently in visitation evangelism—we started home. We had just reached where our car was parked, about a block away, when the maid came hurrying after us. Evidently Don Peter had had a miraculous recovery and would see us now.

Back we went and were shown into the bedroom where Peter was under blankets in the bed. He seemed quite willing to talk with us, but I was concerned about what he might or might not be wearing under the covers, so I asked if Ann could wait for us in the living room.

After some preliminary small talk I got directly to the point, "If you were to die tonight, Peter, would you likely go to heaven?"

He responded with conviction, "Of course."

Then I asked him, "If tonight were the night and you died and found yourself at heaven's door and God asked you, 'Peter why should I let you into my heaven?' what would your answer be?"

His reply left me speechless. Never before nor since have I found myself without some kind of a reply. Peter confided in me with great pride, "God needs me in heaven. You see I am a leader of men, and I would be a great help in getting heaven organized."

It is not for me to say when a confession is genuine or not but Peter definitely prayed to receive Christ that night.

It was after the prayer that we experienced yet another first. While I was leading his wife to a saving knowledge of Christ and focused on that task, Peter was preparing Pisco sours for us all. He strolled into the front room with a tray full of glasses and announced he wanted to propose a toast. At that time, due to Mission rules, we drank no alcohol and found ourselves in a bit of a bind. What he prayed made it easy to decide. Peter said, "A toast to Jesus the Lord and what He has done for my household tonight."

Yet again God took us out of our comfort range into a totally new experience.

Brandon in Chile

Shortly after Brandon came to Chile, we noticed that Piro, our adopted Chilean daughter, was spending even more time at our house! The two of them became almost inseparable, and together they took the youth of the church under their wings. In just a few months they had a group of nearly twenty studying the Bible and eating and then studying more of the Bible.

I am eternally grateful to the God who both drew Brandon back to Himself and then gave me, his earthly dad, the opportunity to perform his baptism; it sticks in my mind as the most significant, the most precious baptism, and the baptism for which I am most grateful. Familiar words I had asked of many others—do you believe Jesus is your one true Saviour?—now took my breath away and caused the floodgates of my eyes to open as I listened to my son answering, with tremendous certitude, "Yes I do!"

The whole church rejoiced, wept and celebrated with us because of his special relationship with Piro and because we were truly all becoming a family. We rejoiced. The Poseck family put on an honorary meal. The entire congregation cried with joy and some of what I just wrote I was only told about after because during the time of the baptism I believe in some way I was so in the presence of God that I was largely unaware of what happened around us.

Multiple Decisions

I remember, on one occasion, visiting an apartment where we expected to meet a man and his wife. When we finally found their place and went up to their apartment, I was really taken aback. There were so many people present that we could hardly get in! I don't remember if we could even all sit. I have a mental picture of sofas and chairs packed deep with people and others standing behind them—eighteen in all!

I had never before presented the gospel to this many people at the same time. God gave me wisdom in terms of how to start and what to do. I began by presenting the gospel to the host extending an invitation to the others that they were welcome to listen in.

"Would you like to receive this gift?" I asked him.

"Yes," he said. "This is what I have been waiting for." He prayed with me, then I prayed for him.

What should I do next? "Is there anyone else that would like to receive this gift?" I asked.

They all said, "Yes," in one chorus. Surely they had not all understood, so I presented the gospel again with even more emphasis on personal sin and need for repentance. Again they chorused 'yes,' and we all prayed together. What an evening!

Finding a Location

The vision we were following was to build a large church on a main street in Santiago. Although this had been successfully done already in Lima Peru, the typical church at that time in Chile was built to house around fifty people and was located in a remote difficult to access area.

Our vision included reaching Chile—all of Chile. This then led to beginning in Santiago because within a hundred kilometre radius of Santiago was to be found nearly eighty percent of the entire country's population, and in the upper class because they controlled the resources needed to accomplish the task. Santiago itself in the 1980s was home to five million. I did the math to see how many churches of fifty people it would take to reach the city and the country and determined there were not enough building materials in all of Chile to accomplish the task.

In November of 1988, the church was starting to get uncomfortable in its new home at the hotel Acacias. It was growing and again approaching the capacity of the largest room in the hotel. Once again the urgency came upon us. We would need to move in order to grow.

Desperation leads to desperate acts. I began, one spring, to walk the length of the main street, Las Condes. The part that ran through our area of town was perhaps four kilometres long. I must have been seen as slightly crazy by some—and a total lunatic by others. I remember asking and being granted a meeting with the ambassador from Great Britain whose embassy fell along that route. They had a large property including an empty lot that seemed to be just inviting a large Protestant church.

This also I believe was part of the new strategy. It is not that others before us had no faith. There are many whose faith far surpassed our little mustard seed, yet *acting* by faith is a necessary part of seeing any vision fulfilled.

We met for tea one afternoon. After exchanging pleasantries, the ambassador who no doubt was expecting something entirely different asked, "How may I help you?"

I took a big breath and began. "Well you see, I lead a growing congregation that plans to build a large church on Las Condes and we need a lot big enough." A pause gave me the chance to bail out but plunged forward. "The embassy has such a lot, and I see it is overgrown and not being used. Perhaps we could come to some agreement?"

He must have been thinking, *Who let this lunatic in here?* In fact it was God's mercy that he didn't take me seriously and ask something like, "How would you like to pay for this land?" Actually my appreciation for the sensitivity of the English grew quite a bit just then. He didn't laugh. He didn't appear to be angry. He stated in all apparent sincerity, "Well, no actually, the property is not for sale at this time."

We both had saved face, and I had done what I believe God had asked of me. The quest continued and I walked the several mile lengths of Las Condes and went into any building that looked remotely like it would be suitable for our needs. I learned so much that spring and summer, including a couple of things about myself—namely, that I am a coward and never feel confident. I was acting solely on obedience.

I learned that there was still a great deal of animosity between Catholics and Protestants. I had several conversations that began well and then changed dramatically when the inevitable came out. I would say we are a religious community. I would observe the hackles go up and would be asked with either distain or anger, "Are you Protestants?"

Then I would be told one of many reasons why they couldn't help. Some were still properly polite; others just showed me the door.

You can imagine that after a couple of months of walking I was getting discouraged. As we entered summer, the temperatures rose, and that didn't help either. By the end of the day, I would be sticky and dirty. In Santiago the smog is so bad that the collar of a white shirt has a deep black ring around it after being worn even once. I felt as if my entire body had a big black stain on it.

Looking back now, I realize that I can no longer conjure up the depth of the pain and the doubt that walked with me during those days. Of course, the story has a happy ending. A miraculous and glorious thanks to God.

Location Found

One day I did find a lot and an owner willing to sell. The lot was being used by a ceramic factory. About this time Francisco had begun to help out at the church, and he went with me to see this property I had located. We agreed it was too small and left dejectedly not even bothering to ask the price because the lot was only about half the minimum size of what we needed.

We got into my car and turned around for the trip back to our house. About two blocks later I heard that voice again. God was speaking. *You need to go back and look at the house beside the ceramic factory.* There was no evidence that this house was for sale but back we went and rang the bell at the outside gate and were let in. I remember the look on the man's face when we asked him if the house was for sale. A combination of anger and fear; you see, he was renting the house, and the last thing he wanted was to have to move. He showed us the way out.

Now the doubts returned. Had God spoken? I was ready to say I had not heard His voice when Francisco said, "Let's go to land registry and see who owns that property!"

A couple of hours later we had a name, address and phone number. The very next day Francisco contacted them. We had learned during this year that, when it came time to negotiate, it was mandatory that a Chilean do it. On the other hand, when we were looking, it was an advantage that I be seen as involved. For some reason they thought, because I was American, that we were millionaires.

Francisco made the call and reported to us so excited that we could hardly understand what he was saying. "You are not going to believe this. Hallelujah! God has answered."

Finally he took a deep breath and slowed down and told us what had happened.

When he contacted the owner, Francisco was not expecting him to be so affable. During his meeting the man said, "How did you find out? How did you know that we are planning to sell the house?"

Let's just say that it helps to have God as your real-estate agent.

God Orchestrates the Purchase

Although the doors to obtain a suitable site on which to build appeared to be opening, the fact remained we had no money and no chance that the Mission would help. About that time, the president of our denomination in Canada made a visit to Chile. He came for two reasons. First because he had never visited Chile and he wanted to meet all the missionaries; secondly, because the denomination had funds left over from the year's end and their policy to start each New Year at zero balance caused them to seek projects that were in need of support. So it was, that in God's perfect timing, we received the majority of the money we needed.

Our plan was to combine these two properties into one land title. If either of the two owners got wind of this the price would jump dramatically. This had to be done quickly and quietly as the united value would be significantly above what they were individually willing to sell for. Of course, we pulled it off, and Ann and I moved into the existing house. Then the next obstacle presented itself.

We had no architectural plans for what we needed. We had an idea of the requirements as far as a floor plan for the church, but how to get plans and how to then have those plans approved by the municipality of Las Condes? Again we were apparently facing a huge brick wall.

Ann and I went on holidays. We truly needed a break. I had come to the end of my energy and was depressed enough that

I was in danger of giving up the vision. We could have sold this land and made enough money to build four or five of the typical churches.

We were absent from Chile for nearly three weeks. I returned with no more idea of how to proceed than before, but I was rested and had hope again. Almost the same moment we got home the phone rang, and Francisco was trying to tell us something but again he was so excited we could hardly understand him.

"I have the plans," he was saying.

"What plans?" I asked.

"The plans for the new church. Come up to my office and see them."

Still unsure of what he was trying to tell us, we went to see him. He sat in his office with a look on his face like the cat that had just swallowed the canary. He pulled out a beautiful pastel artistic presentation of what became the Cordillera Church. Immediately my heart concurred.

"This is it!" It was perfect in every way.

Francisco waited for us to take it all in then began again.

"This is not even the half of it," he said. "The architect is one of the foremost architects in all of Chile. He is recently retired. Amongst his achievements he designed and built the presidential palace!"

Slowly my lack of faith was surfacing again. How could we afford this? Finally I expressed my doubt. "How will we be able to pay this man?"

"Oh," said Francisco, "that is the best part. When I first asked him if he thought he could design a large temple for a Protestant church he became emotional. He replied, 'It is the one thing I never managed to do in my career, and I would consider it a privilege. In fact it will be my pleasure to make a gift to you of a full set of plans together with the approval from the municipal hall, which I will also get for you.'"

Although the actual construction took several years to complete, as far as seeing the vision completed, it was on that day. Our career, however, took a dramatic and unexpected turn that saw us go to Spain and not be able to return to Chile for four years.

Colin is Expelled

Our son Colin is exceptionally bright. For him, the school in Quito was a blessing. In 1989 his senior year he had a teacher who recognized his ability and worked with him and prepared Colin in a unique way to go on to become what he is today, a professor with a Doctorate from McGill University.

Unfortunately, the rest of the administration, including his dorm parents, looked on his exceptional abilities as a threat to the system—like parents like son; we too seemed to threaten the status quo. An example comes to mind. For years the school paper had been dull and of little interest to the students for whom the teachers prepared it. Colin first accepted the position of editor of the paper but found that nearly everything he wanted to write was censored. So he did what Colin does; he found a way around the system, and he started his own newspaper.

It was sufficiently clandestine that it was never officially shut down, but when pictures of the staff were included in one issue, albeit that they all had paper bags on their heads, for Colin the jig was up. Colin is six foot four and towered over the rest of the class. The paper was a huge success with the students, which apparently threatened some of the faculty.

One of the most dastardly things I have ever had to stomach as a parent happened two months before Colin was to graduate from Quito. The dorm parents got wind that some of the students were smoking marijuana. All the students were fully aware of the zero-tolerance policy. If you are caught with drugs you are expelled immediately. Nothing could be proven, so a general meeting was held by the school leaders with the students, and the principal of the school informed the kids that they knew who the offenders were and reminded them of school policy. He then went on to say that a special amnesty was available for any student who would come forward and confess and that those students would be punished but not expelled.

Colin was the only one who went forward. We received a call the next day, letting us know that Colin had been expelled and would be put on a plane back to Canada. I didn't get the entire story for a couple of years, but we were forced to make arrangements within a few hours for our son to return to Canada without us. He had two months left to graduate from the only high school he had known.

Despicable is a word that comes to mind, and I still struggle to repress emotions. This is another blemish on a school that professed to follow Jesus Christ. We were actually contacted later by the school saying they were going to charge us for the school supplies Colin would have used had he finished the year. I then wrote a letter to the Vice President of Missions in South America David Volstad. I received a reply from the Vice President of the denomination threatening me to keep quiet and not to smear the names of respectable people doing a very good job in Quito or I would run the risk of being sent home myself.

PART TWO: Furlough in Canada 1990–1992

Happy News

I remember arriving back in Toronto in November of 1990. It was a time of very mixed emotions. While we were glad to be home—Brandon and Colin both lived in Canada now—our departure had also been a time of mixed blessings. We had decided that the right thing to do in preparation for our absence was to leave the church in the hands of Francisco. Further, we had decided that he would be the head pastor, and we would work under his authority, doing evangelism when we returned.

This decision took all of my conviction. I called a meeting of the entire church and reminded them that I was the head pastor. Then as I had their full attention I said, "It is my desire and my instruction that Francisco be declared the lead pastor and that you all give him the loyalty and support you have shown me." Many tears followed, but God knows the future as well as He knows the past, and He had us take a step that would ensure the life of the church would continue.

Obviously not the entire church was in favour of this move. We were not only the founding pastors, but the spiritual fathers to the majority of the people. Some pleaded with us not to leave, and if we left to come back as their pastor.

We returned to Canada to live in a very nice apartment in Kelowna, British Columbia. During the last crucifixion, the Mission had drafted three conditions for our return to Chile. Only if I sought counselling and submitted to the authority of a local church could we return. Additionally, we were to stay in Canada for twelve months—not the six months that Canada had previously authorized.

I was glad for the counselling. I arrived in Canada pretty terribly beaten up emotionally. As a result of counselling, together with the help of an excellent general practitioner, I was diagnosed with clinical depression. I remember sitting in the doctor's office and being surprised that she spent so much time with me. In a day where you are lucky to see a doctor at all, she spent nearly an hour with me. Near the end she said, "I am surprised you can still function at all, Sir. "

I am ever so grateful that there are still true medical practitioners out there, for in a very real way she saved my life. I followed her advice, and in less than three weeks, I was aware of a change in my demeanour that was every bit as magnificent as the metamorphosis of a caterpillar. Previously I could not see the sun. Everything was being seen through a deep fog. It had grown to be my normal. It was so great to be fully alive again!

Our time in Canada was tremendous. We were truly loved and welcomed by the body of the Kelowna Church. I was given many opportunities to speak in the months I was not on speaking tours. January of 1991, I left for Ontario. I believe I was away for nine weeks. As much as I love speaking, by the end of the time I longed to get home.

For anyone who knows Kelowna, in the beautiful Okanagan valley, you will fully appreciate how much we enjoyed our summer. What is not to enjoy? The lake was a ten minute walk from our apartment. We both grew up in Kelowna, so it was truly coming home for us. In addition, there was an event coming closer and closer that we were all looking forward to. Just prior to our leaving Chile, Brandon had called. "Dad," he said, "I have found the girl I want to marry."

We were delighted, for they were going to honour us by waiting until we were home so that I could perform the ceremony for them in August.

August of 1991 I had the glorious privilege of performing the wedding for our son and his wife Meghan. It held all the promise of being a perfect match. They had met at Bible College and both of them espoused a desire to go to the mission field. In order to accomplish this, they finished that year at Bible College and enrolled in the University of Saskatchewan for the next fall term.

Meadow Lake

The town that without a doubt is my favourite tour town in all of Canada is Meadow Lake in Northern Saskatchewan. Yes, it is beautiful, but we fell in love with the people and particularly one family there that I still count among my very good friends. We felt from the first that we had known them all our lives.

As the relationship developed, they invited us to use their summer cottage on Jeannette Lake in the Meadow Lake Provincial Park. I have memories that span over twenty years with this family. The recollections of the cabin include beginning the training of two of our Airedale dogs. Airedales can be very strong-willed, and when the time comes to introduce them to obedience there is a moment of conflict of wills that must be decided once for all. This is best not done near your house where the neighbours can watch! I love my dogs, and they love me, and sometimes I wish I had trained dogs before I raised my sons!

Part of a day at the lake included at least one long walk on one of the many trails. There were always surprises, which included, over the years, seeing many, many deer. One day I heard a sound I had never heard before and stopped frozen, waiting to hear it again. I did and was able to locate the direction and then saw an enormous horned owl well over two feet tall watching me. He swooped out of the tree, glided away to my amazement without the slightest sound.

We saw bears several times. Once they came up on the deck attracted by the smell of the BBQ. This BBQ was enormous and very heavy, but they did their best to turn it over and get inside to lick the grill. Another time we heard crashing at the next door neighbours. It was late in the fall and most folks had already shut their cabins up for the winter, so we wondered if intruders had come. Quietly we went over to investigate. There were two bears that had broken into their metal storage shed as if it was made of canvas. Inside they were turning over things again, probably looking to get at another tasty BBQ.

Another highlight from our days at camp was learning how to sail. Our host, Merv, gave me lessons and took me out in their laser class boat. Eventually, I learned how to sail by myself, and my graduation test was to sail the length of the dog leg lake— about one kilometre—go around an island at the far end, and return safely to the cabin. That day I passed the test, but I had other days sailing where things did not go so well, due mainly to my inexperience and impatience. There were often days with no wind. Frustrated I would let prudence go if a squall came up in the afternoon. I tried to sail during a storm or two. It is amazing how fast a boat can flip over!

Have you ever sat and listened to the wind? There is little man-made noise at this lake. Many times I would just sit on the porch with a cup of coffee and a book and listen to the sound of the wind in the trees. Each type of tree produces a different sound. It seemed to me to be a symphony of sound, and I loved it.

Our hosts are quite the outdoors types. They are great fish-ermen and know a lot about nature. They introduced us to the world of wild mushrooms. Once hooked on the taste, it became a regular activity to go out during the day to ensure we had a good supply of fresh wild mushrooms to go with our supper. At the same time our stays usually coincided with wild strawberries and blueberries season. The intense flavour of wild berries must be experienced to be appreciated. Of course, they are even better when served with vanilla ice cream.

Alberta

We were now halfway through our year's term at home, and although we still had another tour to do our hearts were turning back to Santiago. As a special privilege the church assigned us both to the same tour. Now the length of the tour didn't really matter; we were together. Off we went in our own car—another concession—to Alberta.

The day before leaving to begin the tour, we received a Dear John letter from the Mission in Chile. We had completed all the terms that had been set out for us, but they were not yet done. "We are so sorry to inform you . . . " the letter began. Pain like that of a cold north wind tore at our souls as we continued. The Mission had decided that we were not welcome to return to Chile. They wished us good luck in our future endeavours and assured us, hypocritically, of their prayers.

Only one very visceral illustration even comes close to describing how we felt: Gutted—like a fish that has just been opened up from gill to tail. We had to leave that same morning in order to arrive in Calgary for our orientation meeting before starting our tour. What should have been a delightful day driving over Rogers Pass, one of our most loved pieces of road, now became a dirge, like going to a funeral.

By the time we arrived in Revelstoke, about an hour and a half from Kelowna, the black had turned to red. In a rage, I said, "It is not fair. We have done everything they asked us to do."

We stopped at a pay phone to call our headquarters located in Toronto in order to talk to our boss.

He had already been advised, and although he was not shocked, he also was angry. But out of his sympathetic heart came words of wisdom. "Doug, you and Ann can fight this. I have the authority to order them to take you back, but do you want to continue on under those conditions?"

He went on to share some information that few others knew of at that time. He said, "In a short time all Canadian missionaries currently in Chile will be reassigned to other countries, so even if you were to go back it would only be for a few years. We would like you to go to Spain. Enjoy your tour. Don't worry about the details. We will arrange things and keep you well informed."

We did enjoy that tour. Both Ann and I were good communicators. That fall the weather was incredible. It stayed warm well into November, and we richly enjoyed exploring Alberta.

Brandon was living in Calgary and Colin came out while we were there on tour. One morning we were starting a day at Heritage Park in southwest Calgary by having breakfast at the Western Café. Just before we ordered, we heard a commotion outside, music and cheering. Out we ran to see. From the wrap-around porch of the restaurant, we saw a horse-drawn wagon appear and realized it was an election campaign. On the wagon was Preston Manning, who was running as the federal head of the newly formed Reform party. We had met him once before and had been invited to his house for dessert.

The wagon pulled up and Preston stepped down. He came straight over to us and asked, "What are you doing here? Aren't you supposed to be in Spain?" We were super-impressed both by the memory and the empathy of the man. He truly cared. In the next months before we left Canada, the Manning Foundation was to donate a sizeable amount towards outfitting us for Spain. The simple note that came with the cheque said, "We hope this will help you find the things you will need for your new home in Spain."

Ann and I had the time of our lives. that November. The weather was fantastic—more like summer than fall—and we seemed to have a lot of spare time, especially in the mornings. We took advantage of it and toured everything within driving distance, including the dinosaur park, Waterton Lakes National Park, the Prince of Wales Hotel, and a special day at Cypress National Park where we almost got locked inside the park—they were closing the gates for the end of the season.

One of the places where we were billeted during our Alberta tour stands out in my memory. With all fairness, I should mention that I am very grateful for all the homes that were opened to us in hospitality, but at the same time, humorous situations did arise. One of these was in a home where we slept in the front room which was part of an open kitchen. The first morning was interesting when the host and hostess arose to get ready for work and began to cook breakfast. In those days the bladder was much stronger, and it's a good thing it was because we were held captive under our covers until they left for work.

Unexpected Holiday

Our year in Canada had now passed, and we still did not have orders to leave for Spain. At first this was not a problem. We were still living in Kelowna, and that was beyond great. Yet the family that had so graciously lent us the apartment for a year was due to return home in the next few weeks. The last report on our visas for Spain was: "It will take a little longer."

It seemed obvious to us that we do something we had never done before. Go to Disneyland. That turned into a trip of a lifetime and was fully attended by God's blessing. In human terms the timing was not perfect. It was late February and the weather forecast for California was not great. In fact that year they were experiencing flooding. We really had no choice; it was now or never.

We thought that perhaps we could see a great deal of Disneyland in three days. I have listened to the experiences of many others at Disneyland. Long lines. Extreme heat. But the weather warnings had kept people away. There were no lineups!

None! We ran from one attraction to the next and climbed on. The weather? Absolutely tremendous. No rain at all. Just perfect. We took it all in. Knott's Berry Farm. Columbia Studios. In addition we visited with family and friends. What a lovely way to "fill in time."

In April of 1992, we said our goodbyes as Brandon and Meghan left for a summer of tree planting. Brandon had been tree planting several times previously so we were used to not having contact with him while he was away planting. This time the lack of communication would shield us from a great deal.

PART THREE: Spain
1992–1996

Mission Politics

Even today I am not entirely sure why we were assigned to Spain and not allowed by the Chilean Mission to return to Chile. Part of me still wants to return to Santiago and help in the church. Yet I am absolutely sure, despite my lack of understanding, that a sovereign God did not make a mistake. That conviction flies full in the face of our early experience in Spain. We were sent to Barcelona because the Mission headquarters was there. The Mission did not know where they wanted us to be assigned. We visited several churches, including Valencia and Zaragoza, while living in a two-bedroom apartment with a single gal missionary who attended the church in Barcelona. Cramped quarters to say the least.

We were attending an evening service in the National Church in Barcelona when things really got interesting. Shortly after the service ended, these two men came and sat with us. Generalities soon became very specific and pointed. The Vice President of missions in the United States asked, "How are you enjoying working in Spain?"

To which we replied, "Well, actually we aren't working yet."

"Why is that?" he asked.

"We haven't received our assignment yet." I am sure, out of the corner of my eye, I could see the other gentleman, the Regional

Director, whose responsibility it was to ensure we were assigned, turn white.

"How long have you been in Spain?" asked the VP.

"Just over six months."

Being a gentleman, and not wanting to put his Regional Director in a bad light, he contained his answer to, "Is that so?"

Not surprisingly, we were assigned to Madrid within two weeks, and also not surprisingly the Regional Director was transferred some months later.

Move to Barcelona 1992

God is always sovereign, even when we think life is out of control such as it seemed to be in the early days in Barcelona. In addition to living in a vacuum, not knowing what we were going to do or where we would be assigned and feeling like we were imposing on a single gal by living with her in a very small apartment with no end date in sight, one morning I received a phone call that no parent needs to receive, ever.

That fateful morning I picked up the phone and heard my son say, "Dad, Meghan is gone." I needed not hear the details as the agony in his voice told the whole story. It was the pitch of a young calf at the moment he is neutered, the voice of one in such pain that the agony is beyond bearing. Slowly he managed to give me more details including how she had fallen into open adultery and then run off with a tree planter she had known only for a couple of weeks.

As I listened, my mind began to think of how to get back to Canada to help him. Brandon said not to come home. There was nothing we could do. Yet here in Spain we were living in limbo. Why not go back? I asked permission from the field chairman and he very gently denied the request. At the time it was difficult for me, but looking back it is likely if we had gone home to help we would not have been able to do much and most certainly we would not have returned to finish what God had for us in Spain. I have told God on several occasions that the cost of responding to the call was too high. This was one of those times.

Summer Olympics in Barcelona

As if God understood that we were coming very close to circumstances that were beyond what we would be able to endure, He provided for us the opportunity of a lifetime—to work in the summer Olympics as volunteers in the privileged area of the Athletes' Village.

This included several perks such as free transportation in all of Barcelona; free food during the time we were in the village; security passes that gave us access to most restricted areas including a private beach; and most of all face to face contact with all the heads of all the sports and the athletes. We literally were hobnobbing with the who's who of the Olympics. Even the athletes could not come into our area!

Much more important, as He has done so many times in our life, He turned this apparent setback into a glorious opportunity and preparation for our future ministry in Spain. We met some very key people; Spaniards who we knew were not easy to get into relationship with.

Once again, as had been the case in Chile, some of our missionary colleagues received us with jaded advice. We heard, "Don't expect things to be like they were in Chile. Spain is different. Spaniards won't come to your house, and never ever will they invite you into their homes."

These were not words of encouragement, but fortunately neither did we receive them. In our simple minds, God is the same—not only yesterday, today and forever. He is the same God in Spain as the God we had seen perform miracles in Chile.

As a direct result of being in the Olympics, we were invited to the home of Fernando, who had been an Olympic archer for

Spain. We met a young Christian couple who worked and lived in Galicia, a province of Spain located on the East coast and up to then just a name. They worked alongside of us for the entire time, and over the weeks we got to know them, appreciate them and to learn from them as Spaniards what it meant to be a Christian in Spain.

Near the end of our time in the Olympics, which had stretched out to over six weeks because we were invited as part of a smaller group to stay on and work through the para-Olympics, we received an offer from this couple that we could not refuse. They had a minibus that needed to be driven to Galicia. Would we consider driving it for them? Sight unseen we agreed. I don't think we ever regretted taking the offer, but it did lead to some interesting incidents.

The bus turned out to be a Bible bus, a mobile library of Christian materials that was designed to include a platform from which messages could be preached. Further, this bus was blatantly conspicuous as it had been painted in psychedelic colours which loudly proclaimed its function. We wondered if we would be stoned crossing this country that had proved itself to be so actively resistant to any form of religious change to the historic Roman Catholic faith.

The next part of the adventure was to discover that the diesel-powered bus was dramatically underpowered. Any slight incline in the road had us gearing down, and if the grade persisted we soon were crawling along with the rest of the traffic gawking at the sight and whizzing past. Some encouraged us with their horns and hand signals.

The North of Spain is so different in every way from Barcelona. I don't think we had yet appreciated that, even to this day, Spain is really an amalgamation of four cultures living in more of a coalition than a unified country. We left Barcelona and the Mediterranean coast with its Catalan language and culture and began to climb up to a plain that is the location of the capital of Madrid. Here the country is rocky, barren and dry; the people speak Spanish with an accent distinct from the other Spanish speakers in Spain.

Not stopping in Madrid, we headed northeast which soon saw us heading towards the Pyrenees that form the border between Spain and France. Soon we were passing through a completely different culture, language and geography; this was Basque country. We then turned east again to head directly towards the Atlantic Ocean and our destination, Galicia. The residents are referred to as Gallegos, and are more closely related to Portugal than to Spain in language and culture.

We stopped to see our friends at the home of his parents and were welcomed as if part of the family. They gave us their blessing to continue using the bus as transportation for as long as we wanted in order to get to know the area a little better. Thinking this to be a

God-given windfall, we began that same day and soon found ourselves having yet another adventure.

We set off to see the world-renowned city—and capital of Galicia—Santiago de Compostela, which is also the third most highly respected religious site for the Catholic Church. It is most known for its glorious and ancient cathedral, but before you can get to it you have to navigate the walls of a city that retains most of its medieval charm—including narrow streets—far too narrow as it turned out for a Bible bus!

Navigating with a tourist map, we set off to get close enough to walk to the cathedral which we could see in the distance. "Turn here. Now turn here." Ann was busy looking at the map; I was becoming concerned with the roads which were getting increasingly narrower.

"Honey, I don't think we can go much further."

"Sure you can," she replied. "I think there is a parking lot just ahead."

Scrape, crunch: the sounds of side view mirrors hitting the ancient walls on either side at the same time.

I confess I lost it at that moment. I tried backing up, only to see a large soft-drink truck pulling in behind us blocking the only way out. Trapped. Stuck. Desperate. And all in a bus painted in psychedelic colours announcing that we were evangelical Christians doing damage to the third most revered place on earth to Catholics!

After I calmed down, which probably only took minutes—but at the time seemed to be several lifetimes—the large truck saw our dilemma and began to back up clearing an escape route for us. We in turn managed to back out of there without causing further damage. The next step was to find a parking lot safe for RVs, and there we left the bus for the remainder of our tour of the spectacular town and cathedral.

Moving to Madrid

Within our first year of ministry in Spain, we were assigned to work in the capital of Madrid. We were delighted and once again faced the daunting task of discovering where, in a city of eight million souls, God wanted us to focus.

This important decision becomes even more critical in a country and city where ninety-five percent of the population live in apartment blocks behind gated guarded walls. God led us clearly to live in one such complex in the area of Mira Sierra located in the north of Madrid. So far so good. If nothing else, from our apartment on the sixth floor, we had a clear, unobstructed view of the Pyrenees. With field glasses we could see the lights of a ski hill in the winter!

We didn't know it then, but we had begun doing what is now called incarnation ministry. This term later became popular and several books have been written on the topic of living the Gospel in community with those who do not yet understand what it means to have a relationship with the risen Christ. We had been advised by several colleagues not to be too hard on ourselves and not to expect much at the beginning. In fact, we agreed with them that generally Spaniards were much more direct that the Chileans we had become used to and thus likely to be overtly resistant to us.

At first their normal conduct was like a slap in our face. In Chile we had grown accustomed to Chilean politeness. Typically a Chilean at your table wanting you to pass them salt or pepper would ask something like, "When you are finished with the salt would you mind passing it to me?" Now we heard, "Give me the salt." Similarly the phone would be answered in Chile with, "Hi, who is it?" Now we heard, "Speak." It took a time of adjustment before we realized the Spanish didn't think it rude but practical.

It is also true that the Spanish are quite old-fashioned and, similar to our British roots, they don't take easily to strangers. You typically must be introduced by a friend before you are accepted. This is a huge problem in a country where you are a foreigner with no Spanish friends.

We undertook to find a way. This began with just putting ourselves in the walking paths of our neighbours. We found out when the mail was delivered to the building and then purposefully hung out in that area so we could see and be seen. We shopped where our neighbours shopped and put ourselves in their path so often that we might have been accused of stalking.

Weeks turned into months, and we had not so much as made eye contact with a neighbour let alone talked to one. But slowly things began to change, and the operative word is *slowly*. One by one, some of our neighbours began to make eye contact with us at the mailboxes or on the sidewalk outside of our building.

Then we got an occasional reply to our, 'good morning' or 'good afternoon'. Nothing as fancy as a full response, but at least a guttural sound or two. The ice had been broken, and this soon led to short conversations and eventually to our first invitation to a neighbour's home.

On the surface, these breakthroughs seemed just to happen, but in addition to much fervent prayer, a rolodex was being developed that within a year contained the names of over sixty of the ninety families that lived in our building. This then enabled us to send birthday cards and seasonal cards to most of our neighbours. Then folks just began to drop in, especially if they wanted some advice on family difficulties. We became safe people to many.

Building a Church

In 1994 we were granted a three-month furlough in New Zealand. This was a generous concession from our Mission for the compassionate reason of my mother living in Auckland. The New Zealand church and its leaders were also very accommodating and granted us many opportunities to minister in most of the churches of the North Island.

One thing that really stands out in my mind is the weekend we built a church. The church in Rotorura planned to build their church on a weekend as a testimony to the neighbours. We arrived early Saturday morning and sure enough, except for the foundations, all that was there was a pile of building materials and a good number of volunteers.

We worked sun up to sun down to achieve our goal. We had our service in the building early afternoon on Sunday followed by a traditional *Hangi*. This meal had been cooking all Sunday to be ready for us when we finished the worship service. A Hangi is a meal centred on pig meat with vegetables cooked in a large pit into which white hot rocks are dumped and then covered with leaves. The result is a succulent blending of the flavours of the meat with sweet potatoes and fresh vegetables and was all the reward we needed in return for the many hours of hard work.

La Cruz

Back in Madrid, we still did not have a full time ministry, other than what we did in the building. We developed a close relationship with a couple from Youth With A Mission (YWAM). They became our spiritual confidants and advisers. This then led to an invitation from them one summer to do evangelism in a small town about an hour south of Madrid called La Cruz.

Ann had her first ride on AVE which is the Spanish high-speed train that runs from Madrid to Seville at speeds up to 300km/hr. Her ride took forty-five minutes while our car drive to pick her up took nearly two hours. We were a team of twelve in all, and we met up in La Cruz. The afternoon we arrived, we went to the city plaza and prayed and praised.

A typical plaza in Spain has on its four sides the authorities of the country. There was there a church, the municipal hall, the police and the judicial building. La Cruz is a small village that has been given historic legal right, because of a sixteenth century proclamation, to still call itself a town. It has renown in Spain as being the last place the Inquisition put a martyr to death by fire.

Before we finished singing I am sure the 5,000 residents all had heard about the foreigners in their town. We were being billeted at the house of someone's relative, and off we went to rest for the next day's adventure.

The next morning around ten, early by Spanish standards, we set our plan to canvass as much of the city as possible and to hand out a pamphlet both telling the locals who we were and that we were going to be having a rally in the city park that evening. We split up into pairs and went off door by door; we were a little hesitant in terms of how we might be received. As far as we could tell, this town—and several thousand others in Spain at that time—had never had one official opportunity to hear the gospel other than via the Catholic Church. The residents knew we were not Catholic, and we wondered how they would receive us. It was not hard to imagine being stoned or run out of town.

We got back together in the early afternoon for lunch. It was a welcome break and it felt good to get out of the hot sun to enjoy a siesta. The whole town was shut down to escape the heat of the day, and there would be no more visiting until four. We then returned to the streets and continued house to house, encouraged by the positive reception of the morning. Not only were we not facing resistance, but the people were helpful—even friendly. We continued as late as possible before returning to our base to prepare for the evening rally.

Rally in the Park

The "park" was really not much more than an undeveloped part of the city with some small trees and a few austere benches. There was some kind of a public building near the middle from which we managed to find electricity and run an extension cord which we would need before we finished.

We began with singing and some skits to draw the young folk who became very curious to get a close up look at *the strangers*. It seemed that none of the adults would venture closer than the outskirts of the park and stood well back, behind the trees.

I don't remember exactly when it was that the local band showed up for practice. Nearly every town and village in Spain has some kind of musical representation, usually related to religious activities. This town sported a trumpet band. We really could not see them clearly as dusk had already fallen, but we could surely hear them. I didn't know that a town of 5,000 could muster so many trumpets! And yes, they really did need to practice. They tooted and marched around the park—literally doing circles around us for some time. We bravely soldiered on in spite of our sore ears.

At some point, I realized that the spiritual realities in this town were manifesting their disapproval at our appearance and our performance. Deep inside me excitement began to rise. We had arrived at the point where our speaker was to begin when two large German shepherds came rushing into the circle of light cast by the single light bulb. We stood in a rough semi-circle, drawing back as they bared their teeth. These big dogs snarled and then for some reason really took after each other. The fur flew for a short time, and then, as quickly as they had appeared, they were gone, leaving us to wonder if they had been real at all.

No matter, our speaker moved forward to the vacated area in the light. He began, speaking by faith to the invisible people we hoped were still standing on the outside of the park—now invisible in the total dark of night.

"We have come to your town of La Cruz to tell you the wonderful news of salvation through Jesus Christ."

I had not thought much about what he might say that evening and even less about how he might conduct the service. He is a native Spanish speaker and spoke very well, and I for one was proud of him. He reached the close of his message and began to give an altar call.

"This is a very important visit as there are many, many other towns and villages in Spain that have not yet received this same news, and it is unlikely that we will return here in your lifetime. I am going to invite you to receive this wonderful gift for yourself."

Then I heard words that made me cringe: "If you sense God moving in your soul and want to receive Jesus as your personal Saviour, I invite you to come from where you are and join us here and kneel with me and I will pray for you."

Oh me of little faith. I thought, *Things have gone so well tonight, Leo. All has been positive up to now. But to have an altar call? This is not ever done in Spain because people do not respond. Further, we have no assurance at this point that people can hear or even that there are people standing in the darkness. This is going to go very badly. Leo.*

Yet before the thoughts were complete in my mind, I began to see movement in the darkness. Slowly shadows became forms and they began to appear as they entered the light to join us. At one point, before they had fully emerged from the darkness, I became aware that I was weeping, then in the same instant I was kneeling just as they were beginning to kneel. The only difference was that they knelt from choice; I knelt smitten by God who was demonstrating to me and to all the others who joined me on the ground that He is Lord of all.

If memory serves, nine young men and women received Christ that night. There are no words to properly describe what happened, much less how we all felt. It is a moment frozen in time. What happened during the next forty-eight hours does give some indication of the magnitude of those events. In less than two days, the entire evangelical community of Spain had heard about what had happened in La Cruz, and in a country where not much positive and visible was happening in the evangelical church there was rejoicing.

In our apartment complex, we became friends with a Basque couple, Anna and Roberto. Their home was Vitoria but they were on a work assignment in Madrid. They invited us, on two occasions, to spend a weekend with them in 'their country.'

A Retreat in Santiago

Sometime in 1994 we received a call from the leaders of the church in Santiago, Chile. They invited us to attend what they described as a couples' retreat. When we pressed them for details they became somewhat elusive, and that annoyed us. Most of these people were not only good friends but had been our disciples. Why would they not trust us, their pastor, with more details? All they would say is that we would have all expenses paid, including airfare.

Needless to say we accepted. This was a very emotional time for us as we had previously been denied permission to return to Chile. This absence of four years had weighed heavily on us although we had maintained contact as best we could via email and occasional phone calls. We were met at the airport as if we were royalty. Yet when anything related to this mysterious couples' weekend was mentioned this same vague elusiveness prevailed.

We were lent a pickup truck to drive for the weekend and given instructions as to where the event was, how to get there, and the time. We found the location easily as it was a convent located in an area of the city we knew quite well. In fact it was a beautiful retreat centre, behind high walls that hid from public view a very nice lawn and garden area. When we arrived, there was already a lineup of vehicles waiting their turn on the street to get into the area. Our turn finally came.

We were mesmerized. Most of these people we did not yet know, but they all acted as if they had known us for many years. We drove in and stopped at the front door of the large entrance to the convent, and it was as if we had entered a five star hotel. Couples came hurrying out to carry our bags; our truck was driven away by a valet. We were checked in and taken to our rooms so efficiently that it no longer seemed we were one of perhaps fifty couples but rather that we had shown up at a friend's house for the weekend and were being shown to our room by them.

The details of these weekends are purposely not fully revealed out of respect for the many couples who have yet to experience the weekend. As it has done for thousands of couples the weekend changed our lives. I can tell you that after the weekend, when we were taken with our bags to our pickup, it had been "decorated" complete with tin cans tied to the bumper. We made quite a sight I am sure: this old couple driving around Santiago with *Just Married* signs painted on our old pickup truck.

The Monday after the weekend we met with Francisco, the pastor of the church, and other key leaders of the ALMA ministry. A question that would both change our life direction and save our ministry was asked. "Do you think this will work in Spain?"

We had absolutely no hesitation. This is a gift from God to enable us to reach Spaniards. They beamed, having come to this conclusion themselves years earlier. They eagerly told us that the program, in its original form, had actually started in Spain.

Over the next few months, we saw the hand of God in the birth of this new ministry. It was, for us, an indescribable joy that

Chileans who we had helped and who had become like family to us were now extending a very tangible hand to help us.

I recount some of the amazing coincidences we began to discover. This ministry had been started and developed by the Catholic Church in Spain—Mallorca to be precise. One of the families we had become close to in our building spent their summers in Mallorca, and their priest had been instrumental in the developing a program to help troubled marriages in the Catholic Church.

Our friends in Chile had, in a round-about way through friends in an Anglican church, been given permission by the Catholic Church to use this ministry tool in Santiago. They changed it slightly and renamed it ALMA, which is the Spanish word for soul. Now a world away, a former colony was reaching back to its roots, Spain, to help.

We began to talk about the details of taking ALMA to Spain.

ALMA in Madrid—Mission Impossible

Again in our lives and our ministry we learned not to ask how, but only to determine if this was what God wanted us to do. The answer was obvious. ALMA would somehow start in Madrid. We had no answers to the multitude of logistical questions. In fact, we had fleeting moments when we were sure we must not have heard correctly, one of them when we began to look for a venue.

If we had thought that Chile was a country with a strong Roman Catholic bias we found out that we were indeed in the country that began the Inquisition and still thinks of itself as the defender of the Catholic faith. Protestants are seen as heretics and not to be tolerated let alone helped. After weeks of searching, we could not find any facility adequate to hold an ALMA retreat.

But once again we were reminded that we serve a sovereign God who opens doors that men cannot close. In the building where we lived, we had met and become friends with a couple who are best described as intellectuals. Francisco was a professor at a university, and his wife taught religion to men who were preparing for the priesthood. It was his priest in Mallorca who had started the ministry that we were going to adapt and use under the name of ALMA. Francisco made a call to a local monastery on my behalf and arranged for a meeting with the man in charge.

Out of this meeting, ALMA was born in Madrid, but not without further testing our faith and resolve. We need to acknowledge that our field chairman at that time took a huge risk with us. We could tell him no more about the program than the Chileans had told us before we attended our first weekend—little to nothing. In spite of this, he supported us. I began then to count the cost, which turned out to be a considerably depressing task. We now had the necessary spiritual and moral support of the mission, but there was no financial support available. We would have to find a way to do this on our own. I calculated that to begin ALMA in Madrid would cost close to $90,000 over a two-year period.

We nearly gave up at this point. I remember that the Mission from time to time gave permission to raise funds for special projects. We soon received such permission. That in itself did little to inspire us, as many people are granted work specials and never receive a dollar.

I am not even sure if we did much in the way of promoting this project to the constituents back home. The time drew near when we would have to commit ourselves to Chile in order for them to arrange for vacation time for every member of the team who would come to Madrid to help us. About a week before the deadline, we had gathered less than a thousand of the needed $90,000. Then one morning our fax machine began to sing. We received a printout of nearly half a page of donors totalling several thousand dollars.

We took this to be the first fruits, and that God would see that every penny needed would be provided, and so we notified Francisco in Santiago to book their tickets.

It happened exactly like that. Each day the list and the amount donated grew. We did not even know the majority of those who contributed. I remember one donation in particular that came from a lady who owned a hair salon in the States. She was not even a member of the same denomination. She never told us how she had heard of our need, only that she had heard from God and sent $5,000 in obedience.

One day we received over three pages of donations! Within a week, the full amount was in and, as if someone had shut off the power, our fax did not run again.

The weekend was huge. In this new conservative Spanish culture, we witnessed the same miracles that we had seen in Chile: lives changed; forgiveness given and received; Spaniards came to full faith. We built a friendship with the priest in charge of the monastery. We know of at least one couple that came Friday with plans made to dissolve their marriage when they returned home on Sunday. Instead of returning home to inform their children of this separation, they asked their forgiveness for not being loving parents and committed themselves to a whole new beginning.

PART FOUR: Canada 1996–2002

Return to Kelowna

In the spring of 1996, a church in Ontario contacted us and invited us to come and speak to them in return for return tickets from Madrid to Canada. Not only was this to be a surprise holiday and something of a victory tour to share the great things that God was doing in Spain, but it would also prove to be the start of a new and unexpected chapter in our lives.

We spoke in several churches on our way from Burlington to Kelowna, where Brandon was living with Granny, Ann's mom. We knew that he was still struggling with the failure of his marriage, and we also knew that he had gone to stay with Ann's mom who was also suffering with depression stemming from her dealing her failing health which had in turn been triggered by the premature death of her son. It was a case of the sick trying to help the frail and aged.

Neither Ann nor I were ready for what we encountered. I remember walking up the stairs to the apartment that Granny had called home for some thirty-five years. We all had great memories of her there. She was the best mother-in-law in the world and the absolutely most encouraging person I have ever met. Yet now, for the first time I could remember, she was discouraged and our homecoming was tragic.

Up the stairs we went and entered into what really was our second home, such was the feeling at Granny's place. The weight of the darkness of depression in that place nearly brought us to our knees. It took all of our experience and professionalism not to cry out aghast. There was no bubbly welcome from Granny. Brandon lay on a couch. When he finally dragged himself off to greet us, we saw how thin he was. Brandon is six foot two, and I am sure he weighed no more than a hundred and twenty pounds. Gaunt, tired, eyes hollow and black, it was not hard to imagine that he was suffering from a serious disease.

After a very strained time—instead of what should have been a great reunion after not seeing each other for a nearly five years—we withdrew to the place we were staying. As we got into the car I turned to Ann. "You know we can't go back to Spain, don't you?"

She nodded with tears in her eyes. We were about to be stripped of another ministry.

Our Mission graciously gave us a six month six-month emergency furlough that we used to begin to deal with the situation, the first step of which was moving Ann's mom into a care facility. During this time, I went on a speaking tour, and Ann stayed home to minister to her mom and our son. It was months rather than weeks before her dedication and love began to show results.

Brandon had been convinced his life was over. In time we persuaded him that his life was not nearly over, and that he could and should return to finish his studies at university. With the help of his mother, he began to fill out applications for the fall semester. Months passed, and there was no reply to his applications. Logic had led us to apply only to universities in larger cities thinking that any ministry we might have would develop more easily in a larger city. Now desperation led us to apply to the University of Saskatchewan, where Brandon had been attending before the tragedy. Almost miraculously they not only accepted him but opened up his file as if he had never dropped his studies five years earlier.

By default, we were moving to Saskatchewan. Our commitment to our son was to provide him a home until he finished his studies. How would we provide? That would be determined later. I was on a tour in northern Saskatchewan when I received the news of his acceptance to the university. The last week of my tour, I was moved to call the pastor of a large church in Saskatchewan who was a long-time friend. I spoke with a conviction that I probably did not feel

"Eldon," I said, "I want you to think about bringing ALMA Marriage Encounter to Saskatoon." Before he could object I jumped back in with, "Don't think about if you can afford it: ask only if God wants you to do it. If you believe God wants it to happen, then it will."

I am sure he was taken aback by both the suddenness of the call and my directness, but to his great credit he was not flustered. "We are having a board meeting tomorrow," he said, "and I will bring it before the board."

In a few days, after I got home, he called me and now he was as excited as I was. "This has never happened before in my ministry. Doug, I told the board about this ministry, and before I could even begin to describe what it might entail they replied unanimously: YES."

Move to Saskatoon.

We began preparing the groundwork for ALMA–Canada. All the details fit easily into one paragraph, but the emotional demand of keeping the vision alive was very demanding. Instead of being in a large city such as Santiago or Madrid, we were proposing beginning the Canadian version of ALMA in a city of which it has been said, "You can't get there from here."

A well-worn joke comes to mind. An American tourist from the south west of the States was going across Canada in a motor home. When they arrived in Saskatoon, they needed directions and gas so they pulled into a service station. The wife reminded her husband to ask for directions while he paid for the fuel. He asked the pump attendant, "Where are we?"

"Saskatoon Saskatchewan," came the reply.

Dismayed he returned to the car. He sat down, a little shaken. His wife asked him, "Well where are we?"

"I don't know, they don't speak English here."

In January of 1998, during this time of preparation, six couples travelled from Saskatoon to Santiago to experience an ALMA Marriage Encounter for themselves. Even at this stage in the preparation process—fully a year—there was enough opposition that the program could have been stillborn.

But God, Sovereign God, began by changing all our lives as we bonded together on that trip. He even arranged for an earthquake! Our dear Canadian friends who had supported us in prayer and financially for all our years in Chile now were experiencing missions for themselves. When we returned home there would be no stopping us.

Later that year, sixteen Chilean couples came to Saskatoon to help us do the first weekend. Most of those dear folks paid their own way as a gift to us all. The weekend was a huge success, and we began to fit into the routine of having three ALMA weekends per year.

The next phase of ALMA is to "pass it on." Just as the Chileans had come and enabled us, we began to seek where God would have us plant ALMA. God was not slow in leading us. I received a call from a pastor I didn't know who had just arrived in Saskatoon and had heard about what we were doing. "Could we do that?" he asked.

We began the process of learning how to enable others which culminated in a successful launch of another ALMA about eighteen months later, including, as a bonus, a huge number of lifetime friends.

Women's Encounter

What would the church do without dedicated women? From the very beginning, the ladies of the church made it known in no uncertain terms that they wanted to start their own Encounter just as soon as possible. In no time, Ann had rallied a group of competent, passionate women around her, and together they made the weekend happen. As always, key ladies from Chile arrived to assist us, but in reality, Ann and her ladies could have brought it off by themselves. My part was to pray and enjoy several nights off while the ladies prepared and worked hard. Thus All Women Encounters (AWE), was born in Canada.

Passing ALMA On

Where next? We were feeling more confident about the how to part of ALMA. When we approached the church in Ontario that had helped us so often and so freely it seemed to be a natural fit. Eighteen months later we sent a team of eighteen couples to Burlington. Another successful launch.

Thailand?

Several months passed, and we were getting no clear sense as to where the next ALMA launch should take place. Then during the summer of 1999, I received a phone call from the States from a fellow called Dick who began to ask me questions about how to start ALMA. I was intrigued and gave him some information and he agreed to look at it and call me back

A couple of days later he called to say he was ready to make the commitment and to sign the agreement. Then he revealed that he was a missionary to Thailand, living in Bangkok, and that he was only home on a short furlough. I should have been concerned and perhaps responded with common sense, which would suggest that starting ALMA in Thailand was not a good idea, but I was certain that God was in this.

White Elephants

I doubt if the others were as confident as I seemed to be. The idea of starting in Bangkok had some serious, inherent problems. If I had not been as sure then I would have not been able to answer the questions that would soon be coming. *Did I think that a marriage program based on Christian Judaic principles would work in a largely Buddhist country? Why did we choose a country so far away? The transportation costs would be prohibitive. Remembering that a large number of our couples paid for their own travel, would we get sufficient numbers to help do the first weekend?*

The answer to the last question was a resounding yes. In fact, we had to limit the number of people who wanted to go and pay their own way, and in retrospect, the Bangkok ALMA is among the most successful in the entire world, having themselves now multiplied into Cambodia and the Philippines, neither of which are Christian-based cultures.

The next stage in developing the program was to invite key leaders from the Bangkok church to come and experience an ALMA weekend for themselves. For some of you, the mere mention that the weekend the Thai leaders attended in Saskatoon was in January will cause you to smile. If not then let me tell you about a winter sleigh ride we took them on.

We wanted to give them a true taste of Canadiana and particularly the Canadian prairies. Members of our church graciously volunteered their farm and facilities to that end. This family raises work horses and has a huge barn that houses them in the winter, and over the barn is an upper room designed for parties and dances. We would treat them to an old fashioned sleigh ride followed by an authentic country barbeque in a barn!

The evening of the sleigh ride was not particularly cold by our standards—probably no worse than minus ten. It was a clear night with little wind, and we though it ideal for a sleigh ride. We found suitable clothes to fit our diminutive guests. We then waited at the front door of the main house for the horses and sleigh to arrive.

I observed that the four Thai couples had huddled together and were talking to each other. I moved a little closer and, despite of the language barrier, it was very clear what was on their minds. They all thought they were going to die! Freeze to death actually. For my part, I knew that would be impossible, for I knew what they had on. One I had witnessed put on long underwear, pants and a flannel shirt. Over that he had a winter parka and a snowmobile suit. He was wearing a toque bound around with a huge scarf. Only his eyes were visible but they told the story. There was terror in those eyes.

I believe they truly enjoyed the ride, and it was a perfect night. The stars on a clear night on the prairies are brilliant and of course the Northern Lights. A night to remember, and it was not half over. Our hosts had arranged a true country banquet. The main table groaned under the weight of food. Much to the delight of our guests, there was a huge potbellied stove up there and it was more than warm; it was hot.

The ALMA weekend was especially spectacular. Thai people are culturally very reserved, partly because they are Asian and partly due to their Buddhist heritage. We began to see at that weekend what we have observed at every subsequent ALMA weekend in Thailand: that God is bigger than culture, and that when He touches a heart it shows even on the outside.

I am quite sure that, before the weekend finished, each of the four couples had resolved that ALMA was necessary in Thailand. God, however, had a couple of surprises left for us all.

Mondays after an ALMA weekend are used for debriefing. We gathered that day with our friends from Bangkok for breakfast. We also spent time answering questions and developing the vision of the ministry in more detail. As we suspected, they were already convinced.

After breakfast, we gathered together for prayer. We had done some preparatory work in terms of what was proper in their culture and had clearly learned that physical touch was to be done with great care and that we were never, ever to touch their heads.

They sat in a circle facing each other, and the team gathered around them and we began to pray. Prayer is a basic tenet of ALMA. It is not a token thing, but rather an essential foundational thing. We were prepared to pray for some time.

Earnest prayer soon was being made by many. For my part, I could not concentrate. I was seeing a picture of an elephant in my mind, a white elephant. I could hear voices praying, but I could not hear words. Finally I blurted out, "Is there some significance to the word elephant?"

One of the Thais answered with much emotion. "The elephant is the symbol of our country."

"Does it make any difference that this elephant is white?" I asked.

Now they were in awe, for they revealed that a white elephant is sacred and a symbol of family unity. Then they began to shake as the Holy Spirit descended on us all. There had been no doubt regarding starting ALMA in Bangkok before, but now there was an eager excitement to begin as soon as possible.

ALMA Bangkok

We arrived in Bangkok at midnight. It was a Wednesday in January of 2001, about six months after the weekend in Saskatoon. Our team of seventeen couples stepped off the plane into what was to us a suffocating heat and were met by smells and sights that none of us had ever experienced before; our senses came alive. It was to be a time we would never forget.

Another basic tenet of ALMA is that the mission is paramount. We do not allow for recovery from jet lag or fatigue. Time is of the essence, and Thailand would be no different. It is our norm at these times to be sleep deprived. No one complains, in fact, it seems to help with unity, harmony and efficiency as we all make allowances for each other.

First, the weekend. I think this was the first time ALMA International, which operates in over fifteen countries, had ventured into a nation with no Christian orientation or tradition. No one knew, at this time, if we could relate—if the people would respond or, for that matter, if anyone would come.

We were greeted at the airport as if we were royalty. Such love, care, respect as we have not experienced before or after. The weekend began Friday evening. All that could be done by way of preparation was done. The only thing remaining was to pray that the couples would come. They came! And they responded to the care and attention like all the other couples we had received, in Canada and in Chile. They came with the same cautious look in their eyes—*what have we gotten ourselves into?* They responded as all others do to the love, and before many hours, they began to trust the team and to entrust themselves fully into our care and the purpose of the weekend—to strengthen their marriage relationships.

To describe the weekend in detail would take hours, but to give an idea of what happened differently takes only one illustration. To those who know there is a spiritual world which is invisible to our eyes and recognize that there are opposing forces in this world, the story will make immediate sense.

ALMA is based on Christian teachings and values. There is no attempt made to change those values. The only concession is to try and make them culturally relevant. At some point during a session on Saturday morning, one lady bolted. Members from the team went immediately to help her. She did not want help. She was out of control, screaming and running to get out of the building. I sensed the seriousness of this, and while we were accustomed to people needing a "time out" from the emotions of a session, this was far more than that. Here was a huge spiritual war. Slowly I caught up to the small group of ladies who were trying their best to calm and control the lady—she was now trying to run out into the middle of a freeway that ran past the front of the hotel into what would have been certain death. Already I knew there was no social or emotional answer to what I was witnessing and began to pray.

My prayer took a turn towards warfare as the woman, now almost foaming at the mouth, reached out and clamped her teeth into the hand of one of the women.

"In the name of Jesus, I command you to let this woman go."

As if a tap of rage had been turned off, the woman's demeanour changed totally. She became docile and somewhat confused as if it had been someone else doing the running, the screaming and the biting. Things returned quickly to normal. The weekend was a success. We were witness to things that none there had ever witnessed before. I remember a man telling his wife, I love you, out loud and in public. In the Thai culture this would never happen. It was very common—nearly an absolute truth in Thailand—that men do not tell their wives they love them. Perhaps one time during courting but never after. As this weekend closed, it was common. When a woman ran to her husband and leapt into his arms and hugged him as if in an embrace of death, all of us who were present smiled and recognized that the same God who blesses ALMA in other countries was now blessing it in Thailand. Then we wept tears of joy for the reconciliations and families being restored.

Golf Banquet

One of the displays of honour and gratitude was a banquet put on for the entire team at one of the most prestigious golf clubs in Bangkok. We arrived at the very swanky club and entered by climbing a magnificent tier of beautiful wood steps into a sumptuous lobby. There we were greeted by our hosts, Doctors Satien and Apiluck. Dr. Satien is a personal physician to the king of Thailand. After an official welcome, we were shown into a banquet hall and shown to our assigned seats.

If you have ever been to an oriental wedding, perhaps you have some idea of the dining we enjoyed that evening. Were there seven or eight courses? I am not sure, but I remember that any two of them could have been considered a fine meal.

Appetites totally destroyed, the evening's program commenced. Speeches of gratitude, testimonies of lives changed. We had come to Bangkok to work, and from the time we stepped off the aircraft Wednesday less than a week earlier, we had slept probably less than ten hours each. Our bodies ached with fatigue while our minds played tricks on us due to jet lag. All of this was washed away in the glory of that evening. Not very many humans, even once in their lives, get the opportunity to see that much positive change in that short a time.

The speeches ended with a time of exchanging gifts, which is a tradition in the ALMA program. Our small gifts were given with much love but paled in comparison to the gifts we were receiving from our new Thai friends.

Then we went golfing! Can you believe that? Of course it makes total sense in this country of extreme heat and humidity to golf at night but, until that moment, I had no idea that golf courses with full lighting existed! Tee off times started at ten at night! To make a perfect day even better, on the taxi ride back to the hotel, at around one in the morning we had to stop and yield to an elephant—only in Thailand.

Most of us had made plans to stay for a week after the ministry was done. Our hosts arranged for several days in the south of Thailand in a well-known resort area. We stayed in a first class hotel only a short distance from one of the most amazing beaches we have ever seen. There we began to catch up on our sleep and surrender to jet lag. What a way to go!

Drive Home and Mad Driver

There was some mix up with our bus driver who had been contracted to drive us to the resort and back again to Bangkok. Evidently we left a couple of hours later than he was expecting. Dick, our guide, had had words with him and he had become sullen. Ann and I sat in the front seat directly behind the driver. All of us were now relaxed from our down time and ready to sleep on the four-hour return trip. Most did sleep blissfully, ignorant of the drama that we were witnessing.

Of course we understand no Thai at all. But body language is international and needs no translation. The driver was beyond ticked. I would say he was close to possessed by his rage. He began to bumper ride every vehicle he got behind. Remember we were traveling in a huge tour bus. The roads in the south are by no means freeways and, for the most part, are narrow two-lane highways. Soon, not content to bumper ride and wait for either the vehicle in front to pull over or to wait for an obvious place to pass, our driver began to pass everything in front.

For us, sleep was no longer an option. Prayer became the main focus of our lives for the next few hours. I do not remember how many close calls we had—they were too many. I don't remember how many times when we were passing that I could not see the road under our wheels and expected at any moment to roll over and crash in the ditch. I do remember thinking that it takes a long time for a tour bus to pass as I counted the seconds from when we pulled out until when we pulled back into our lane. I do remember a surreal kind of peace. *Que sera sera*. We had no option but to trust in the God of creation to watch over us. We could not stop the man because of lack of language. In fact I feared trying because he might take his concentration off his driving, and I would then have actually caused a disaster.

Goodbye Thailand

We were given a send-off at the airport that we would never forget. I believe that the entire Thai team was there, all thirty-six of them. They had prepared banners, and as we took group pictures together with the Canadian team of thirty four it caused a lot of attention. Then it was time to go through security. Tears prevailed. Cries from both groups of, "We will never forget you," rang out. We gathered silently in the waiting lounge, each with our own memories. Full to overflowing with joy and just as full of a desire that it had never ended.

Snow Storm in Tokyo

On our second trip to Bangkok in January of 2001, I experienced fear in a way I never had before. Leaving Bangkok for home, the only thing on our minds was the sorrow of leaving those dear people and the sublime joy of the memories we had created together. The topic of weather never crossed my mind until we were getting close to our stop in Tokyo. First, the captain reported that they were having "weather" over the airport. That was no big deal. When he came on a little later and advised there was heavy snow falling over Tokyo and that there was the slim possibility that we might be turned away to an alternative airport the announcement fully had my attention. Up to this time the flight had been nothing but smooth sailing.

The closer we got to the airport, the less we needed to be told the weather was deteriorating because the plane was beginning to be tossed around. I was seated next to a young entrepreneur who had been in Thailand buying jewelry to sell back home in the States. She was very nervous and began to sit with her knees under her as close to the fetal position as a seat belt will allow.

The plane began its decent. Visibility was zero; a full blizzard was raging outside, and it made things very precarious that the wind was blowing across the runway. Now my co-passenger was moaning and wailing. "I don't want to die. I don't want to die."

I was temporarily distracted by trying to assure her of something I no longer believed myself. "We are going to be OK."

Then abruptly, at about sixty feet off the ground we could see that the plane was making its approach at nearly a forty-five degree angle to the runway because of the gale force winds. *Oh my God, even if we land, the wheels are going to come off this plane,* I thought.

Credit the pilot and his unusual skill that we landed, wheels on. We were the last flight to land or take off for the next twenty hours. Our problems were far from over.

It was night when we landed, probably about five p.m. We did not have the full story about our delay at this point. The announcements began to come, telling us that all flights were delayed until the runways were cleared of snow. We Canadians knew that until this huge snowfall ceased that the one snow plough they have in Tokyo airport would not be getting that job done any time soon.

We had been in the air for over five hours, and we were getting both thirsty and hungry. At first we grumbled when we looked at the prices! A small bottle of water was four dollars. Then we discovered that all concessions close at ten because of airport restrictions. The Tokyo airport closes due to noise restrictions from ten at night until eight in the morning. At least now we knew where we were going to spend the night. For most of us, the small Asian-sized seats on the plane seemed like a comfortable paradise in comparison to sleeping on the floor of an airport.

Needless to say, the next day we missed our connection to Saskatoon in Vancouver International airport, but we were all glad to finally get home having shared an adventure of a lifetime.

Returning to Chile—August 2001

Taken from *A Heritage of Miracles*

Tuesday Aug 21 1:30 p.m. Toronto time in the Toronto airport. 1st flight over—3 more to go! Don't worry! I won't give a flight by flight description, just to say, for now, were on our way!

We have entered the Spanish world—I'm so glad we can understand. Air Canada landed in concourse G and LAN Chile flies out of concourse A, and they are located at opposite sides of this huge airport— probably over a kilometer. We have just traversed this incredible distance. We rented a buggy and took the elevator to the 3rd floor where there are moving walkways, so it was relatively painless—good thing because my carry-on seems to be getting heavier!

I also forgot to mention that a friend drove us to the airport and dropped us off, and two of the Presenting couples came to see us off—at 6AM! We were very touched.

Wed Aug 22 4 p.m. Argentina time! We're here in the apartment of Walter and Estella and their three delightful kids—Samantha, Jessica, and Christopher. The last time we saw Christopher he was only a few months old, and now he's almost 13! That's a long time for a friendship to keep flourishing. We've had lunch a nap and showers. It's 20 °C and brilliant sunshine—so much for the cold winter we were told about!

Thursday Aug 23 2:30 p.m. This morning Doug & I went for a walk in the beautiful warm, fresh spring day. The leaves on the trees are budding, and the birds are busily building nests. We walked to "Parque Savedra" and sat on a park bench in the sunshine and watched the dog-walkers care for their dogs. People live in apartments and work, so they hire someone to walk their dogs. We watched two fellows and a gal walking around fifty dogs in total. The three of them were visiting, and so were the dogs! Some were tied on long leashes to trees nearby, some walked around with long leashes, and others ran free. I guess the walkers know which dogs will run away. In the whole bunch, we only saw one Airedale. All told we saw seven walkers—dogs and humans were enjoying the spring day.

We slept in till 9:30 a.m.! What a treat. After such a long trip, it was wonderful to stretch out.

It takes an adjustment and is hard to realize that we did the same i.e. left the apartment yesterday at 5:00 and went shopping. Walter and Estella had some items to exchange and we tagged along to a huge shopping center. Prices here are not cheap anymore. Argentina is in tough shape.

Anyhoo we had a cappuccino coffee while out, then home for supper at 10:30 p.m. In bed at 11. Everyone was gone the next morning by 8 a.m. Doug and I didn't even hear them leave! The Spanish is coming back pretty easily.

Friday Aug 24. Today is a cloudy day. Doug and Walter went for a walk with that (to me) foul tasting "mate," and I'm just about all packed and ready to go to Chile.

Yesterday we went downtown with Estella—we just love this city! We parked the car for three hours and then walked and walked—down the famous La Florida pedestrian walk-way (mall) across the 9th of July avenue (worlds widest street). The prices were a little cheaper here but still very expensive.

We got home waited for Sammy (Samantha their twenty-one-year-old and oldest) to get home from teaching English (9 p.m.) then went out for supper. A trip to Argentina is not complete until we've had our tummies full of Argentine beef! Now we can leave content!

Sunday we're waiting, all dressed to go to church. It's freezing and damp—I even have Doug's under-shirt on!

Yesterday we had a good old Chilean breakfast— warm bread, cheese, ham and freshly squeezed orange juice and strong coffee served with hot milk. We had showers—the skill of getting hot water from the cali-font came back quickly. Then our host, Dario, took us to Apumanque (shopping center), and I bought postcards. Later I looked high and low and couldn't find the list of addresses I had made. There were sales galore, and so for the first time in eleven years, I bought a pair of black shoes, low heels to replace the ones I bought in Chile before we left!

When we got back we ate "lunch"—it's the big meal—soup, bread, mashed potatoes, barbecued ribs and dessert! We said no to coffee because we already were late for the first event we were scheduled to observe. I wrote notes on "how to" do all that we saw, and I won't bore you with those details except to say we started at 3 p.m. and we finished at 8. Then we went to Janette and Neftali Mollers for supper, and Adolfo and Marlis were there too.

Thursday Aug 5:30 p.m. Cold as usual. Damp as usual. I don't remember it being like this—I do remember cold but not this dampness—however, it has rained every day!

Sunday was the kind of day that words can't express—the joy of seeing so many we've never met before. Eduardo Valderrama so dear with his little baby boy saying to me, "your grandson."

After church and of course one of the last to leave we went with Francisco and Sonia and their whole family (Tiago, Patty Sophia, Angela, Juan, Sonia's mom) to "Pollo al Cognac." That's a wonderful tradition! The huge bowls filled with chicken that has been stewed in cognac, French fries, warm bread, chicken canapé and any kind of wonderful Chilean bread you could ever want! We got "home" at 6 p.m. We stayed with Francisco and Sonia Sunday, Monday and Tuesday night in their one hundred-year-old house in the country! It's still on the outskirts of the city, but the city is beginning to encroach. They are widening the highway, which means they'll end up being only two properties away from the highway. We had a heater in our room!!

Sept 5 Tuesday. I can't believe it! The Canadian youth came on Thursday; the Youth Encounter was Sat. and Sun. Finally the sun came out on Mon. just in time for a glorious trip to the coast. Now today is sunny and the first day we could sleep in. So here we are—in the sun, catching up on reading and writing and trying to get some tan back!

Luckily I have our schedule somewhere which details Mon., Tues. and Wed. It was cold and damp and raining until the kids came. Then it was only cold and damp. Today for the first time they should be able to see the mountains! We met them at the airport on Thursday and they went "home" with the people where they were billeted. For lunch Brandon came over here with the Mollers. There were others here as well for a Peruvian meal. (I like Chilean food better). Thursday evening at the church there was a welcome for the Canadian youth.

Sept 6 Thursday. I'm sitting in a sun spot in a tower! We are at Lee Cave's in Valparaiso in the turret of their huge home on a hill overlooking Valpo and Viña as far as Con Con and Reñaca. I can see a naval ship going by just by glancing up from this page as I sit on the oh-so-comfy bed.

We had empanadas at a farewell party for the kids on Tuesday night, and then on Wed, Coty (our hostess) drove us to the metro, which we took to the bus station and then got a bus to Viña, where Anderly picked us up. We drove by the new condos/apartments where she and Iain will live and drove around seeing all the new developments, then home for lunch and an exquisite visit in her beautiful cozy English home. We also went over to Iain's fabulous home next door and saw the wedding picture of the daughter of Anderly's cousin—a very social event with Prince Charles and Prince Harry and Camilla Parker-Bowles in attendance. Both the bride and groom have published books (we saw them with the personal note inside) Anderly let us pick out one of her paintings to take home, which I just love!

Then Lee Cave picked us up @ 5 p.m. and we went to "the Mall." It's new since we were last here and fabulous. They have managed to keep the stairways and escalators all with a view of the ocean on one side and Viña on the other. Doug wanted a wool sweater and all the sales were on (50% off—end of winter) and he bought two. When he took them to the till they gave him another 25% off—so he got them both (100% wool) for $15. You can imagine how overjoyed he was. We had a "café cortado" there (espresso) then home to our tower and got settled. A bathroom has been installed, so here we are in our own little hideaway with our view!

Thursday in Viña, Lee Cave took us to Zapallar with Carmen Neary, and we ate at the ritzy restaurant on the beach—"Chiringuitos." We finally had our delicious and favourite "machas a la parmasena" and "congrio a la margarita." Delicious! It was the only beautiful, warm clear sunny day of our stay in Chile, and we sat outside enjoying each other's company, the food, the scenery... and an exquisite jewel of a memory.

That evening, Andrew came for supper (roast beef). I did not sleep well that night, but that doesn't diminish the shining day.

Going back on Monday, we slept in and hung around the "parcela" of Francisco and Sonia, and in the evening we went to the church for a welcome supper for us. As the meal went on, folks got up and shared memories of their times with us. We sat with our former neighbours, Victor Manuel and Maria Theresa Esnaola so we could visit because we knew we wouldn't have any other time. She is younger than me and 8 months ago had a stroke! She can talk now, but her right arm is useless and she walks with a limp. We also sat with Verena and Fernando Carmash whom Doug married in Temuco about twelve years ago. Piro was with us (we didn't know her whole family was coming) and Olga Commandary. These were all special folks that, in past time, we had visited but knew we couldn't this time. There were one hundred there—that's more than the church was when we left eleven years ago!

Tuesday was our visit day! We came in to Santiago with Francisco, and he dropped us off in time for lunch with Ofelia accompanied by her daughter Alexandra and her two daughters, Nichole and Michelle. We started looking at old photographs—quite a trip down memory lane as we saw ourselves seventeen years ago when the church started.

Then Alexandra drove us to Piro's for tea. We (she) talked for well over an hour before Scarlette came with her youngest and then Oscar and Chichi. We only had about an hour with them all together before Marcela picked us up and took us to her place for tea (again!) and to visit with her mom and dad. Then she took us to Francisco's office where we met Francisco and he drove us back to his house. We had to stop on the way to pick up his daughter Angela from the hospital where she works as a med student. Then believe it or not we had supper! It must have been indigestion because we were hungry!

Sunday Sept 9. On the way home! This is now airport writing. We left Chile last night. Francisco drove us to the airport, and just before we left, beautiful Maria Pilar and Roberto came to see us off. I've got quite a cold (getting better), so I was too tired to get really emotional.

So now, to fill in the gaps!

On Wednesday we came back to Santiago with Francisco. We worked with him at his office on YES! details then went out to lunch with him. He took us back to our hosts. That night we went to a prayer meeting for YES! And then joined the church's prayer meeting. It was super having another chance to see folks again. Early Thursday the kids came. The welcome at the church was a little stilted—the Canadian kids didn't really know each other, they were cold, felt awkward not knowing the language and a bit leery of Chilean style hamburgers! Francisco in his welcoming speak assured them that their farewell the following Tuesday would be entirely different. He was right! The kids were mingling, hugging, laughing and hoping they would see each other again. The Canadians were happily eating empanadas and were no longer freezing! And we "Old guys" were loving them all!

Back to Friday, that was the tour of Santiago, planned and led by Ivan. We met at the church took the bus down town to the Moneda and went in. When we lived here, under Pinochet's dictatorship, the public was not allowed in to see the government offices. So that was a first for us too.

Brandon had use of our camera, but he did agree to a few historic family photos of AB & D together in Chile after eleven years!

We then walked to the Plaza de Armas and went into the large cathedral. When we came out, there was a huge crowd on the other side of the plaza in front of the municipality offices cheering as the mayor of Santiago gave the keys of the city to Zamorano—the Chilean soccer hero. The whole Chilean national team was there (Brandon was delighted!). It was a great experience for our Canadians! Then we walked to the Mercado Central and went in for lunch. Now that was a shock for the kids! Some were afraid of the seafood, and some were afraid of the dirt! (sawdust floors) But we got them settled in and ordered "fish and chips" for everyone (except one seafood coward who had chicken!) From there we walked to Santa Lucia—the hill where Pedro de Valdivia founded Santiago in 1546. It was great fun watching friendships form between the Canadians themselves as well as with the English-speaking Chileans. We had to climb to the top, but the group pictures were worth it! Then down again and across the street to the market. The kids bought wool toques, ponchos and sweaters and after that they felt a whole lot better (warmer!)

Then we took the subway back to the church. That was another "bonding" experience as Ron (the other adult) didn't move fast enough and the subways doors closed in front of him. We watched in dismay as he was left standing on the platform. We all got off at the next station and waited for the next train. As it sped into the station we waited and watched until we would see Ron (luckily he is tall) and then we all ran like mad and jumped into his car. We were all so relieved to be together again!

At the church, the kids went off with their "parents" and Ron, Doug and I stayed behind to watch the set-up for the Encounter to start the next day. No details there! Except to say that we left around midnight—frozen to the core and doubtful that chaos would ever end. But! When we came back on Saturday at 7:30 a.m. all was done.

The Encounter was spectacular! On Monday, a busload of us went to Viña. It was a holiday, so lots of the English-speaking Chileans came. It was sunny!

We first went to Valparaiso and went up the funicular [electric tram] to the top of one of the 10 hills that make up Valpo. We strolled, looked at the view, took pictures then walked down the hill to the harbour, where we rented a boat and had a guided tour of the bay. It was lots of fun—I just loved the time with Brandon—watching him being so personable.

After the tour, we traveled by bus to Viña and lunch, then back in the bus to the BEACH! The kids had so much fun taking pictures of each other with their feet in the Pacific Ocean, even in winter!

After a leisurely stroll, we got back in the bus and went to the Ostlies for empanadas. Doug and I were so surprised that they lived half a block away from Anderly! So we together with Brandon excused ourselves and went to visit her. She was home and graciously received us. I was so glad she got to see Brandon! (She told us on Tuesday how delightful she found him)

Then we set off for Santiago. We made pretty good time, considering that half of Santiago was returning home after a long weekend. We had one "incident"— as we were driving up a hill we heard what sounded like a rifle shot. The bus stopped—it could have been a flat tire? However, it had been a rock that had been thrown and broken the lower corner of the windshield. While we were by the side of the highway a car also stopped, also hit by a rock. Apparently someone was protesting this new holiday that replaces Sept 11, the day Pinochet took power. Chile's politics are always simmering just beneath the boiling point.

On Tuesday we slept in, and went to the Mollers' for lunch—seafood! Oh joy! And "alcachofas!" (artichokes) Brandon ate two! Then he and Heather went to Maria Pilars, where they met all the other youth and went up to San Cristobal, where they finally could see the Andes. We stayed and visited with Jeannette (Neftali had to go back to work) and then we walked with her to Providencia, where we bought our Chilean wine. Then we had to say goodbye. That always hurts me. We walked down Providencia to Francisco's office where we met with him, Pepe and Erika, Ron and Tim Greenfield (who translated for Ron). Details for YES were finalized, and then Pepe and Erika drove us to the farewell party that I already mentioned.

So that's the gap! And that's the end of the trip letter. In 6 more hours we'll be home, and no p.s. means all went well.

On the trip from Santiago to Miami we each had a little TV screen in the back of the seat in front of us—so besides eating and sleeping we watched two movies of our choice!

OK now I'm napping (we're on the plane, and Doug is already asleep)

Bye bye! Hello normal world!

In less than three years, ALMA Canada had multiplied the ALMA ministry twice in Canada and now oversaw our third, which we had named "our Thai baby." However we knew there was yet much more to do, and the time came again not to rest on our laurels and move into the fullness of ALMA that includes a separate experience for youth.

Youth Encounter with the Spirit (YES)

The acronym to be used for the youth encounter is YES, Youth Encounter with the Spirit. Again the job of preparation began with a trip by the future leaders of Canada to experience a YES weekend. This weekend meant more to Ann and me than any of the others before or since.

With the passing of time, Brandon had recovered almost completely from the deep depression that he was caught in when we returned to Canada from Spain, and his physical health had totally returned, and he was his usual robust self. But he had not recovered at all in his spiritual life. He was still very angry with God. He would not talk about it and had made himself emotionally distant from us.

He lived with us at the time in Saskatoon and he was party to our plans and preparation to go back to Chile. That summer, as usual, Brandon was off planting trees. I had previously talked to him about going to Chile with us, and he had made it quite clear that he didn't want anything to do with the church. "If you pay my way I will go," he said, "but I won't have anything to do with what you are doing." It was quite clear.

Youth Encounter and Brandon's Re-Encounter

We had met Pepe and Erika at the Cordillera church on our last trip to Chile. They headed up the youth Encounter program and gave us their complete support together with a commitment that, when we wanted to start in Canada, we could count on them and their team.

The day to begin YES arrived. We took several of our young leaders with us to experience for themselves the YES weekend in Santiago. During the year of preparation we had talked to Brandon openly about our returning to Chile and again offered him the chance to go with us. We had only one condition; that he attend the YES weekend. His "Not interested" was adamant. However, just as adamant was the prayer of his mother that God change his heart and mind.

One morning shortly before we were due to leave for South America, God nudged me to call Brandon. To fully understand what a God thing this was, keep in mind the chances I would actually be able to talk to him were slim and none. He was tree planting and worked in the bush for weeks at a time. In the unlikely possibility that I got through to him he had made it very clear he was not interested in going to Chile with us. There existed the real possibility that he would be angry with me, thinking I was pressuring him. Regardless, I obeyed the prompting of God.

I got through to him on the first call. It was as if he was waiting for my call. He sounded like a different young man and now was eager to go and eager to go through the YES weekend. We needed yet another miracle. Ann and I were leaving for Chile in less than a week. Brandon was tree planting in British Columbia. Brandon resolved one of the questions immediately. "Dad, we are going on a break in a few days and will have the time off."

I then asked, "Is your passport up to date?" It was. We booked his passage and then made arrangements for him to get his tickets and we left ahead of him.

That YES event, of all the years of ALMA and the many other life-changing, transcendental happenings, stands alone in my mind. We watched God perform His will that weekend. Brandon arrived in Chile. To our eyes his attitude had not changed. He was still politely distant. The weekend began Saturday morning, and Ann and I were given the privilege of watching the entire weekend. This was done only as a concession to us and the fact we were going to be starting in Canada. Many exciting things were happening. We watched the Spirit of God moving in the lives of the future Canadian leaders of YES—though our eyes were really fixed on Brandon. We prayed and we prayed and we prayed. We were expecting that God would soften his heart and restore his broken heart and spirit.

Nothing happened Saturday, or Sunday morning. We had reached the last event of the YES weekend. A time where the youth can share what has happened, what has been their experience. We heard Pepe, the leader say, "We have time only for three more testimonies." We found it in our hearts to thank God just for the fact that Brandon was there and that he had experienced firsthand this emotional weekend.

Then at the last moment, Brandon leapt up and ran down the hall past the some 140 other young people sitting on the floor and jumped up on the platform. I need to digress briefly to help capture the impact of what had just happened.

At that moment in the weekend I was in an adjacent prayer room on my knees. I could not see, only hear. I missed the sprint to the front. Ann told me later that her heart nearly stopped.

Most of the people in the prayer room were folks that knew us very well and also knew, in detail, of Brandon's tragic breakup and subsequent bitterness. When we heard on the loud speaker, "Hi my name is Brandon," the room froze in time. Not a sound was made, for the moment seemed somehow sacred. He continued, "Many of you know me and what I have experienced. Eleven years ago my wife left me, and I reacted badly. I never stopped believing in God, but I told him to go off in a corner of my life and not to bother me. This weekend I have invited Jesus back to be my Lord and to have first place in my life."

The prayer room erupted into sobs of joy and gratitude. I will never forget what God did that day, and He and He alone knew at that time the importance, for only God knew that Ann already had terminal cancer in her body.

Why Ann?

The pain is still excruciating at times. Even now I have to discipline myself to fend off the question my mind puts to my spirit, "Why?" The illness caught us all by surprise, but of course it did not surprise our God. We thought we were coming back to Canada to look after our family. God knew we were coming back so that Ann could die at home with her sons, family and friends.

July 2001, we had just returned from our second ALMA weekend in Bangkok. Ann was in a wheelchair recovering from a hysterectomy. We returned on a real high. Our "Thai baby" was growing fast and would soon be an adult raising a family of her own. In fact, Thailand has been parent to two other ALMA programs proving, once again, that God does know best and that common sense is not necessarily the best way.

YES in Canada

Immediately after our return, we threw ourselves into the last preparation for the first YES weekend in Canada. On the fourth of January, a team of sixteen Chilean youths would arrive, and there was much to do to get ready. A couple of days before, Ann was beginning to show signs that all was not well. She was having huge headaches, but as usual she didn't complain, nor did she let them stop her. What did slow her down was a growing paralysis in her leg. She was stumbling noticeably. The day of the YES weekend, we decided that it would be best if she didn't go, and we arranged for a dear friend to spend the night with her while I went on with the program.

Early into the first night of YES I received a call, "Doug I think you should come home. Something is seriously wrong." It didn't take a doctor to confirm this was serious. The paralysis had progressed to the point she could barely walk and it now affected her left arm and her speech.

As an aside, the YES program was hugely successful without us. For a time Brandon, our son filled in until permanent leaders were trained. Although it is one of the aspects of ALMA that I have had little hands on, it is in my opinion the most dynamic and has the most impact of all ALMA ministries.

First thing the next morning we went to emergency. If you still have confidence in Medicare in this country, it is most likely that you haven't really needed it. By now Ann was in agony and nearly fully paralyzed. We still had to wait, hours as I remember. Finally our number came up and we saw the nurse in charge of triage. Curtly she asked, "What is the matter?" Ann began saying she had a severe headache. "Do you drink coffee?"

"Yes," Ann answered.

"Have you had any today?"

"No," Ann replied.

The nurse rolled her eyes, stopped writing and said, "You have a caffeine headache. Go home and have a cup of coffee."

As soon as I got home I called our family doctor again. I had talked to him the evening before and he said go to emergency first thing in the morning. When I recounted our morning experience he also became very angry. "Let me make a couple of calls," he said. He called us back early in the afternoon to tell us to go back to emergency, but that this time they would expect us.

We didn't have to wait in line for long and Ann was taken in for an MRI. She came back down, and we waited together sitting on her bed in emergency. As we waited together we both received the peace of God together with the absolute knowledge that she was not going to recover from this.

Not long after, a doctor poked her head in. She had tears in her eyes and before she could say anything my dear Ann was comforting her.

"It isn't good news is it, dearie?" I heard her say.

Choking back tears the doctor said, "No it is the worst news. You have three tumours on the right side of your brain that are causing the problem. They are malignant and we do not know at this time if they are primary cancer or metastasized."

Our learning curve about cancer would be abrupt.

"What we do know," she went on, "is that if the tumours are not removed immediately, you will die in a few days." Later that day we were assigned a bed in a ward and our vigil began. The paralysis was nearly complete by this time. Ann could hardly talk and could no longer walk. Things were progressing far, far too fast.

We sat together on the hospital gurney holding each other. I somehow found the strength to speak into the situation what we both knew to be true. "Honey, for all these years we have been teaching people how to live for Christ: now we have been given the opportunity to show them how to die for Him."

Our church family rallied around us. We were given all the help we could possibly have wanted, and none of it was invasive. We felt loved and cared for. We had been told the operation would be performed that evening. Evening turned into night, and after some pressure, we were informed that the OR was particularly busy, and there were some emergencies ahead of us. I wondered what could be more serious than tumours that were likely to kill my wife in the next few hours if they were not removed.

Night passed into the next day and still we had no news. Then we heard that the doctors had been operating for too long and they could perform only one more operation and there was another emergency and another patient. They would have to choose. We prayed fervently. Around 2AM Ann was rushed up to OR, and we rejoiced and prayed even more fervently. These surgeons were going to remove tumours from inside her brain. They were exhausted. We prayed they would not make a slip or a mistake.

That night her life hung in the balance. The best we could say come morning is that she was still alive. The doctors would only say, "We have to wait and see." Then as the hours passed, her vital signs began to improve.

As the days turned into weeks, she began to improve. At one point in February, her exercise regime had reached the point she could walk up and down the basement stairs six or seven times without a break. In spite of what we knew in our soul, we began to allow a new optimism into our hearts. It seemed like she was having a miraculous recovery. Should we begin to praise God for a healing?

All too soon, reality imposed its unwelcome face into our lives. Ann's pain slowly began to increase until I could not control it at home any longer. I was afraid that I would kill her with an overdose of medication. We admitted her to hospice. Two months earlier Colin had returned home to spend time with his mom. Now the three of us the three of us shared the vigil.

I was very concerned about the amount of pain she was experiencing. After a couple of weeks of watching her suffer, I asked for a consult with the doctor in charge of pain at the hospital. The morning before I talked with him, I was in the room with

Ann when she awoke. As sleep yielded to consciousness her pain returned. "Honey, what is your pain level today?"

With no sense of desperation she calmly said, "It's ten, Doug." I learned that such was the pain that the very air in the room caused her bare skin to hurt. As I sat later weeping with the doctor and discussed the reality he nearly broke down. He repeatedly said, "In all my years, I have never seen anything like this. I am so sorry."

The only time Ann had any relief from the oppressive and debilitating pain was when she slept. We agreed to induce sleep for a couple of days to give her relief, hoping that when she awakened we would be more able to deal with her pain.

The night before she died, I knelt in desperation and agony at the side of our bed clutching as it were the horns of the mercy seat. *Oh God, please spare us this trial. Nevertheless, if You decide to take Ann home, I will love You and serve You for as long as You let me live.*

She never woke up. Colin spent her last night with her. He called us around three a.m. It was the 20th of March. "She's gone, Dad."

I had lost my partner of nearly thirty-six years. Less than seventy days from diagnosis to death. Long enough to grieve together; long enough to enter fully the reality of what was to happen.

The church, in which we had served nearly six years, continued to care for me. They graciously did not demand much of me for the next year; I could not have done very much regardless. I was emotionally bankrupt. I was under the care of an excellent counsellor, who made sure that any thoughts of suicide were only fleeting. During this year I was not convinced that I could survive such pain, and I believed I certainly would never marry again.

Reflection

Certainly the ending of this story could seem tragic. It is far from that although pain and sorrow have been constant companions. I lived through the stages of grief stalling for several years in depression.

But God who has never failed me again provided for me in a way I could not have imagined possible.

During the last weeks of Ann's life while she was in hospice a dear friend came to spend time with her literally not leaving her side. We had met Nancy back at the beginning of our journey in a small Bible study group in Calgary in 1976. She and Ann had been close friends ever since.

About a year after Ann's passing Nancy was in Saskatoon—her home town—and called to see how I was doing as we were both still in mourning. After a lunch together at a local restaurant I drove her back to her friend's house. What happened changed my life—again. It was a cold January day and I didn't even volunteer to get out of the car. As she walked past the front of the car, God spoke to me, "Doug there goes your next wife"

I had no feelings except confusion, yet now after ten years of marriage to this wonderful gift of God I say, *thank You.*

As I write we are preparing to take on a new challenge, a new ministry and explore new frontiers. When we follow God, even when we don't fully understand the why where how of the thing we can be assured of a life of purpose and provision.

I wish you all God's best.